GHOLDY MUHA

Unearthing Joy

A Guide to Culturally and Historically Responsive Teaching and Learning

SCHOLASTIC INC.

For AL-WAHHAAB (The Giver of Gifts)

To the ancestors and the land in which this work
was created of Kiikaapoi (Kickapoo)

Senior Vice President and Publisher: Tara Welty
Editorial Director: Sarah Longhi
Editor-at-Large: Tonya Leslie
Development Editor: Raymond Coutu
Senior Editor: Shelley Griffin
Production Editor: Danny Miller
Creative Director: Tannaz Fassihi
Interior Designer: Maria Lilja
Cover and Chapter-Opener Illustrator: Elizabeth Montero

Photos ©: 31, 38 (top, bottom), 43–44, 66–67, 92, 112 (top, bottom), 197: Library of Congress; 35 (top, bottom): horst friedrichs/Alamy Stock Photo; 36 (top): talentbender/Getty Images; 36 (bottom): Duke University; 37 (top): photo-fox/Alamy Stock Photo; 37 (bottom): steeve-x-art/Alamy Stock Photo; 41: Internet Archive; 63: Schomburg Center for Research in Black Culture, Manuscripts, Archives and Rare Books Division/The New York Public Library; 64: Rosena Disery/New York Historical Society; 68: Thomas J O'Halloran/US News & World Report Magazine Photograph Collection/PhotoQuest/Getty Images; 71: LumiNola/Getty Images; 74: FG Trade/Getty Images; 76: kate_sept2004/Getty Images; 113 (top): Yolanda Sealey-Ruiz; 113 (bottom): Marc Royce/Corbis/Getty Images; 120: California Digital Newspaper Collection; 121: Wavebreakmedia/Getty Images; 125: Mayya Abdullayeva/Dreamstime; 140 (kids): UrchenkoJulia/Getty Images; 140 (diet): bit245/Getty Images; 140 (sugar cane): Designer_things/Getty Images; 140 (sugar cane): ONYXprj/Getty Images; 140 (map): mapchart.net; 164: FatCamera/Getty Images; 166: David Fenton/Getty Images; 207 (top, center, bottom): Artwork by children at The Williamsburg High School of Art and Technology in Brooklyn, New York; back cover: Jamal Jameel. All other photos © Shutterstock.com.

Additional Credits: 24: "The Nature of This Flower Is to Bloom" from *Revolutionary Petunias & Other Poems* by Alice Walker. Copyright © 1973, 1972, 1970 by Alice Walker. Used by permission of HarperCollins Publishers; 29: "Oppression" and "Freedom", 59: "Joy", 89: "Life Is Fine", 203: "Bouquet", 217: "I Dream a World" from *The Collected Poems of Langston Hughes* by Langston Hughes, edited by Arnold Rampersad with David Roessel, Associated Editor. Copyright © 1994, 1951 by the Estate of Langston Hughes. Used by permission of Alfred A. Knopf, an imprint of the Knopf Doubleday Publishing Group, and by permission of Harold Ober Associates. Additional poems by Langston Hughes: 117: "Dream Variations", 145: "The Dream Keeper", 175: "Our Land", and 203: "My People". 153: Lyrics from "Cultivating Genius Anthem" by 80's Babies reprinted courtesy of Dominique Jackson. 199: "Art Is a Powerful Tool" by Emory Douglas. Copyright © 2023 by Emory Douglas/Artists Rights Society (ARS), New York. Used by permission.
All rights reserved.

1 2 3 4 5 6 7 8 9 10   40   31 30 29 28 27 26 25 24 23 22

Scholastic Inc., 557 Broadway, New York, NY 10012

Contents

Acknowledgments

A teacher asked me what I was reading while writing my first book and this one.
I responded:

"I was reading the world and listening to the earth."

And when I was, something beautiful flourished—music and melodies with and without words.

I have such beauty in my life. In acknowledging and honoring the humans who have helped to make *Unearthing Joy* as a creative work possible, I draw from the musicality and joy of Stevie Wonder and dedicate songs and lyrics to my village.

This book is for my water, my husband, Dominique "Dee" Jackson—and to my flower, my daughter, Jayla Jackson, who both help me to grow and sustain through the wind and difficulties. You help me to listen to the softness of the earth. Dee, I love that we met through music and your artistry of 80's Babies, and your album, *UnLearn*. You are genius, joy, and consciousness. Thank you for helping me to think through the artistry of this book. You and Jayla unearth the joy inside of me and make this earth a beautiful place to dwell and thrive. You are the "Sunshine of My Life."

To my entire family, you are my "Summer Soft." You stay with me and encourage me through the seasons, starting with the spring—the season I came onto the earth. In the *morning rain*, when I would dance and smile as a little girl, you embraced my joy. In the *winter wind* and *morning snow* and changing leaves in the autumn, you stayed with me.

To Mom and Baba, "As," *around the sun the earth knows she's revolving… I will be loving you always*. Evelyn (Grandma), on your 95th birthday, I asked you what you want to be remembered for on this earth—you answered: That I have loved everybody, even those who did not love me back. You are love and *I'll be loving you always*.

My Sisters and Brothers, "I Love Every Little Thing About You."

Akilah, *my first teacher*. You teach me everything through the waters—still.

Trudie, *big, big sis*. There has never been a day when you haven't started with love.

Abdullah, *my first student* when you allowed me to pretend to be a teacher as a child. Thank you for always supporting my dream and never dimming my light.

Hessom and Armon (Michael), my baby brothers. You are my newest joys. When I met you, you were everything I have been waiting for. Your hearts are so beautiful, and I am thankful to be your big sis.

My bonus brothers, Salah, Abdur-Rahman and Muhammad, mother of Dr. Ajile-Rahman and Grandma Bernice—*until the rainbow burns the stars out in the sky (Always).*

Yolanda Sealey-Ruiz. You are the model of what humans should be on this beautiful earth. You are light. You are my best friend. Thank you for the joy and inspiration and for reading each draft and each idea as I strived to create something that would make our ancestors proud. Thanks for watering the earth with your joy, love, and patience. I know you love the song "If You Really Love Me," and there is no moment that passes where we don't remind and tell each other, "These Three Words." Thank you for purely and *really* loving me through it all.

Jennifer Boykins, thank you for introducing *Cultivating Genius* to Scholastic. I have never left your presence and have never felt a greater sense of love, ease, and joy. You radiate love and you "Send One Your Love."

Tonya Leslie and Ray Coutu, thank you for moving this book to "Higher Ground." Your reflection and feedback have been tremendous and helpful. The unearthing of your creative insight elevated this work.

Cassandra Falcon, "Signed, Sealed, Delivered, I'm Yours." You have helped to move my work forward in ways I could not do alone. I could not do my work without you. I hope you deeply know that. You get stuff done and teach me how to take care of myself and be unapologetic about that self-love time. Thank you for giving so much of yourself.

To the "Golden Lady," Qur'an Shakir, my sister in Islam who helps to keep me connected and grounded to my one true purpose. Every time you step into a room, your golden-ness is at the center.

Chelsey Culley-Love, when I think of you, I think, "Isn't She Lovely?" Thank you for your love and loveliness. You are the epitome of joy.

Saba Vlach, your sisterhood and friendship are love. You are a plea to the people. You remind me of the love we need to see in the world because "Love's in Need of Love Today."

Muhammad Khalifa, thank you for being my brother in Islam, mentor, and friend, and for all the freedom dreaming of improving schools—"If I Ruled the World."

Cynthia Dillard, thank you for teaching me to always (re)member and stay true to my joy. When we are in each other's company, I feel the spirit of "Don't You Worry About a Thing."

Valerie Kinloch, my sister. Your "Visions" will continue to shake up the world. You are the educational leader to lead the masses (and me).

Bettina Love, my model and my sister. When I first heard you speak, I said, here is "Another Star" who we have been waiting for. You continue to teach me, inspire me, and love me each day.

Billye "Sankofa" Waters, I had the opportunity to break bread and reflect with you during my writing. This helped me to discover "Yester-Me, Yester-You, Yesterday."

Auntie Marion Johnson, "I Never Dreamed You'd Leave in Summer." Thank you for your kind and gentle heart. May paradise be all you desired.

Imam Nadim Ali, thank you for being a North Star in my life and of the jumah. You kept reminding me that "Tomorrow Robins Will Sing" (even when I didn't see it). And indeed, they sang.

Scholastic Team, this was a new and creative project, and you created spaces for my ideas and genius to shine. Thank you for your trust in me and our partnership. This book is for you today and tomorrow. "Joy Inside My Tears."

My Brothers and Sisters in Education ("Black Man" and "Black Orchid"): Adrian Dunmeyer, Ahkillah Johnson, Alexis Carella, Allison Curry, Andrea Davis Pinkney, Angel Acosta, Angela Fortune, Antero Garcia, Aria Razfar, Ashley Jackson, Ashtria Scott, Basheer Majeed, Becca Woodard, Beverly Tatum, Bilal Avant, Bilal Polson, Bill Shubert, Bisa Butler, Bobbie Turner, Brent Gilson, Bryan Crandell, Cara Tait, Carry Chan, Chantee Earl, Charity Gordon, Charlene Rowens, Christina Rose, Cornelius Minor, Danny Martin, David Castillo, Deangleo Blanchard, Dena Simmons, Derrick Barnes, Destiny Tripplett, Detra Price, Diallo Hill, Diane Tiche, Dom Belmonte, Douglas Edwards, Duane Davis, Ebony Wilkins, Elise Wilson, Ernest Morrell, Ethan and Ester Clybourne, Ethan Trinh, Fatima Morrell, Francheska Starks, Gertrude Tinker-Sachs, Glenda Chisholm, Gloria Ladson-Billings, Grace Player, Gwen Benson, Harlan Hodge, I.E. Jackson, Islah Tauheed, Ivelisse Ramos Brannon, Jacqueline Rosado, Jamal Cooks, James Anderson, Jamila Lyiscott, Janice Ross, Jeff Garrett, Jen Rowe, Jennifer Banks, Jennifer Esposito, Joe Rumenapp, Joy Valentine, Joyce King, Judy Smith, Julia Torres, Jyoti Kaneria, Kamaria Shauri, Karen Proctor, Kathryn Chval, Kyra Narain-Lloyd, Lali Morales, LaTasha Mosley, LaTavia Bowens, LaToya Teague, Lee Gonzelez, Lester Laminack, Lois Bridges, Maal Jackson, Maima Simmons, Malissa Mootoo, Maria Muhammad, Maria Varelas, Marion Brooks, Mary Neville, Melba Cleckley, Michelle Sanchez, Michelle, Zoss, Mike McGalliard, Nafis Muhammad, Natalie King, Natina Hill, Nathan Phillips, Nickolaus Ortiz, Nicole Yarde, Nya Muhammad, Nychelle Toussaint, Pam Lovett, Pat Kilduff, Pat Wong, Pier Junor-Clarke, Princeanna Walker, Qiana Cutts Givens, Ray Jackson, Regina Bradley, Rich Milner, Richard Haynes, Rosalyn Shahid, Sabrin Abedin, Sakeena Everett, Shamari Reid, Shameka Gerald, Shana Abolafia, Shaneeka Favors-Welch, Sherell McArthur, Sheryl Wilson, Sonia Nieto, Sonja Cherry-Paul, Stacey Franklin, Stacey Joy, Stacey Owsley, Stephanie Graham, Susie Long, Tamara Wells, Terrie Muhammad, Thaione Davis, Tiffany Nyachae, Tisha Ellison, Tonya Perry, Towanda Harris, Tracey Flores, Twiyale Roberts, Yaribel Mercedes, GSU, UIC, Black Teacher Collaborative and YELLOW Teams. I know this long list is still a short list, so to all others, thank you for helping me to find "A Place in the Sun."

Pharrell, when I heard Stevie Wonder's song "Power Flower," I thought of your beautiful voice. Thank you for using your genius to create spaces of education that can be a model for others to build. Thank you for your humanitarian work of YELLOWHAB. Thank you for your creativity and joy to the earth.

Stevie Wonder, what song of yours can I dedicate to you? I choose, "For Your Love." I first heard this song when I was a high school student. You taught me love, and it is through this love that I knew I could do anything, including impacting education. You made me feel that I can do anything and consequently, "I glow, I glow."

To all the educators, podcasters, leaders, and members of teacher organizations, and so many others, you made *Cultivating Genius* feel like my "Song in the Key of Teaching." When I wrote it, I knew it was special, but could not have imagined the love back. To anticipate such love would be a beautiful thing. Thank you, teachers, and leaders, for showing up each day for our children and our communities.

I want to give you your flowers every day.

I want to sing and dance with you. And rejoice in your genius and joy.

Foreword by Pharrell Williams

What is joy? What does it have to do with education? Dr. Gholdy Muhammad has written *Unearthing Joy* to answer those questions and provide a guide to centering joy in PreK–12 education (and beyond). In doing so, she reminds us what it is to smile and play, what it is to love learning, and what it is to be human. I've always said that what makes you different also makes you special, and feeling special can lead to joy. Joy is a special enlightenment. When we are enlightened, we become interesting and we glow. We must enlighten in our schools, teach in exciting and appealing ways, to produce joy. Joy is also collaboration and congregation. It is coming together to learn in unique ways, tapping into each child's potential. It is the celebration of music, art, and creation.

In this remarkable sequel to her bestselling book, *Cultivating Genius*, Dr. Muhammad encourages teachers and school leaders to cultivate joy in themselves and in the beautiful humans they serve. Schools should be spaces of joyful manifestations, where curriculum, community, and consciousness uncover what makes each student special.

For me, joy is also uninhibited, undistracted, euphoric. It means living free to define yourself and realizing your personal and professional dreams.

For me, joy is also uninhibited, undistracted, euphoric. It means living free to define yourself and realizing your personal and professional dreams. Schools are morally obligated to create conditions for joy and to fertilize and cultivate opportunity.

With *Unearthing Joy*, Dr. Muhammad offers a practical path for schools to do that. She not only acknowledges the pursuits that are significant to education, including identity, skills, intellect, and criticality, but also centers joy as the overarching pursuit that inspires all others. Dr. Muhammad believes that all children have innate genius and joy, and she invites us to think about joy in all its dimensions—spiritual, temporal, spatial—despite, or perhaps because of, perennial challenges in PreK–12+ education.

Sometimes, we cannot see joy because we may doubt its existence in such a harsh world. In my design of YELLOW's first micro-school, YELLOWHAB, I conceptualized a space to celebrate belief in possibility and transformation for historically marginalized children who have not received fair access to opportunities to flourish. At YELLOWHAB, the children embark on an educational journey that opens them to foundational knowledge, care, love, and the joy of learning. I don't want children to begin to have an interest in education when they leave school; instead, I want children to have a love for education from the moment they enter our learning spaces. I want them (much as I did) to look over their shoulders at their constellation—at their North Star, at their shiniest points—our teachers. My teachers pointed me to "go that way," without knowing where I was going, but they knew I needed to keep going. They were my form of encouragement, and that is what our children need of their teachers today.

Schools must not only create a joyful ethos, but also sustain it to activate the human spirit.

I recognize the power of looking for joy and creativity in the beauty of the earth and cosmos, in my collaborations with others, and in the power of belief.

The expansive beauty of the cosmos fills me with joy and makes me hopeful about education. I envision the cosmos as a portal of possibility for our roles in joyful education. Teachers can serve as constellations, North Stars, or sources of light to help students 1) become aware of their genius; 2) know they are limitless; and 3) experience joy at school because they are free to be their best selves. Schools must not only create a joyful ethos, but also sustain it to activate the human spirit. All the shining stars in my cosmos were my teachers, and the cosmos came to represent for me the unlimited power of music, the voice of the galaxy, so to speak, that everyone can understand instinctively. In essence, each school should center the joy of the cosmos within its walls, which then, through deep belief, dissolve as physical boundaries to release the potential of each child's spirit, wherever it may go. If you want to see and believe in the infinite possibilities of education, just look up at the night sky, look at nature, look at the goodwill in humanity, and you will know.

When I reflect on my musical career, I feel a rush of immense joy. There is joy in recognizing that all I have can be nurtured and fostered to unlock true, unrestrained potential. What all children have been given as potential can be unearthed into limitless power. I see the process of unearthing as discovery of what is already within. It is unveiling the experiences that are revelatory to the lives of our students. It is the gift. For Dr. Muhammad, this is the hope and future of education, that educators unearth and become self-aware and aware of the genius and joy that already exists on this earth. Dr. Muhammad asks educators and leaders to become conscious of what lies within children, ready to be unearthed for a boundless growth. That unearthing can lead to revelations and agency that fosters a fully joyful human.

I see the process of unearthing as discovery of what is already within. It is unveiling the experiences that are revelatory to the lives of our students. It is the gift.

In *Unearthing Joy*, Dr. Muhammad emphasizes the power of agency as a way to help children own their narratives and futures. We all would benefit from more agency to awaken from our constant state of *sleepwalking*, of dysconsciousness, and grow aware of new ways to reach into and grow from the cosmos and the earth. Children urgently need agency ingrained into their young minds, so they will always hold fast to the power within them and reach their full potential. This journey of growth, as eloquently described by Dr. Muhammad, will reward both educators and students in their collaboration and celebration of a joyful education.

INTRODUCTION

Watering the Earth With Educational Excellence

LAYERED PLAYLIST

Stevie Wonder songs that inspire me about the earth and excellence in education. Play them as you read the Introduction.

"Black Orchid"

"The First Garden"

"The Secret Life of Plants"

"Tree"

"Outside My Window"

"Power Flower"

"A Seed's a Star/Tree Medley"

I remember the exact moment I was introduced to Stevie Wonder's album *Journey Through the Secret Life of Plants* (1979). I was instantly enthralled, as if he had created a gift just for me. Yet I knew Stevie had created something special for the whole world to receive. I thought, "A whole album dedicated to plants and gardens?" I was intrigued and drawn in by the music. Some songs were instrumental, illuminating the sounds one might imagine when watching plants grow. I remember closing my eyes and imagining what flowers would sound like as they grew tall—as they bloomed. Perhaps I connected to each track because my name, *Gholnecsar*, means "sharing flowers," and comes from Persian roots. I like to believe that we often become our names.

I was captivated by Stevie's intentional departure from more typical music with this album. I thought about the genius of artists who use their creative sensibilities to stretch beyond standards and the limitations of the mind—beyond practices that have become normalized. He didn't ask for permission to disrupt music standards of the time, nor was he motivated by album sales. He was, instead, motivated by humanity.

It is that humanity that gave the world (and me) the sounds, movements, and embodiment of plants, flowers, and growth. It was just what the world needed then and what it needs now.

When I listen to each chord and each sound, it feels like joy. And not joy that is merely celebratory or fun, but joy that brings calm and ease—joy that radiates peace. I feel beauty, and my senses experience the aesthetics of a world that sometimes moves so quickly that we humans forget to pause and observe. I feel the earth and humanity at the same time, intertwined.

As I write this introduction, I am listening to "Black Orchid," which Stevie Wonder wrote for the soundtrack of a documentary film he

A NOTE ON LAYERED PLAYLISTS

Unearthing Joy's introduction and each of its chapters begin with a "layered playlist." The songs on each list are intended to be played softly in the background, as you take in the words. Music is special and has a way of helping us to understand a complex world. Each playlist is not meant to be exhaustive nor definitive, but rather connects to the meaning of the book's content—and you should decide on a version of each song that gives you comfort and joy.

couldn't physically see, yet with each track, one could feel his understanding of the beauty of plants on earth. "Black Orchid's" opening lines remind us of a "a new way waiting to be born, in a world with need for change." In the next line, Stevie Wonder juxtaposes love and hate, and the force of wind that is "asked to wait." I listen to those words over and over and think of the state of education and a new direction for our children. That new way, I argue, is culturally and historically responsive education (CHRE).

Revisiting Genius

In my previous book, *Cultivating Genius*, I used *literacy* and *education* synonymously to detail that new way of teaching and learning, which is grounded in and responsive to the histories, identities, literacies, and liberation of children and the social world. I listened to teachers who often said to me: "I understand the need for and meaning of identity, justice, and equity, but what does it look like in a lesson or unit plan, given the constraints and mandates I'm facing, such as test prep in my district?"

Because *Unearthing Joy* picks up where *Cultivating Genius* left off and extends the ideas in it, I recommend reading that book before you read this one.

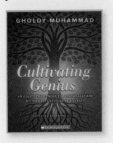

I also listened to children who expect something more from us—they want a better world and expect schools to help them build it. They seek a radical departure from education that ignores or reproduces hurt and harm to society and self. In *Cultivating Genius*, I asked educators to return to brilliant, loving, justice-centered ideologies, and past pursuits of learning and themes of teaching that have been forgotten, hidden, or erased. Dr. Cynthia Dillard (2022) names that shift as the act of (re)membering, which means going back (and back again) to the historical brilliance of the past to better understand and (re)write education today. (Re)membering is a recursive process of writing and rewriting systems, frameworks, and practices. *Cultivating Genius* is a book that moves toward this (re)membering, (re)covering, and (re)writing. To understand equity, justice, and excellence, we must (re)member the triumphs, leaders, and ancestral genius that were rarely taught in teacher preparation programs.

I define *genius* as knowing who we are and *whose* we are—knowing social-emotional intelligence and knowing how to make ourselves smile. Joy is the embodiment of sustained happiness and having knowledge of the world—centering wellness and the gifts that may or may not be captured in traditional school assessments. Conventionally, *genius* is a word that has been applied to a few among us who took one IQ test that was initially developed within a system of marginalization and misrepresentation of children. Asa Hilliard, who remains a leading thinker and cultivator of education, once said:

> I have never encountered any children in any group who are not geniuses. There is no mystery on how to teach them. The first thing you do is treat them as human beings and the second thing you do is love them (Watson-Vandiver & Wiggan, 2021).

Hilliard expressed that belief regardless of what we know or *think we know* about children. If we do not center their gifts, we should not be the ones to teach them. For so long, children have had their stories told from deficit perspectives. They have been identified for what they "can't" do instead of for who they truly are and what they are truly capable of. In fact, many professional books are written in the context of "children and failure." If we are not centering children's humanity through love, there is no strategy, no professional book or instructional method in the world that can prepare the teacher to elevate the child.

When we fail to begin with genius, we risk what Chimamanda Ngozi Adichie (2009) calls "the danger of a single story," which robs families of their dignity and breaks their spirit. For example, she explains that if children continue to hear negative labels or comments spoken about them, they can begin to internalize such negativity and see themselves in deficit ways—this breaks the spirit and joy of so many children and can make them feel worthless. I have never met a child without genius, but I have met children who come to my classroom feeling discouraged by past teachers who have focused on failure rather than growth.

One of the United States' platforms to measure "growth" and "failure," the National Assessment of Educational Progress (NAEP), also known as the Nation's Report Card, provides data on fourth, eighth, and twelfth graders' performance in reading and mathematics. Year after year, results indicate that the United States struggles to educate our children, especially Black children (who we fail the most, according to NAEP). For example, data from 2022 shows that 33 percent of all fourth graders were proficient or advanced in reading, and 37 percent were in mathematics. The reading scores show a decrease of 2 percent from 2019 and the math scores show a decrease of 4 percent, both years very low (U.S. Department of Education, 2022).

Proficiency in reading is defined as being able to integrate and interpret texts and to apply understandings of the text to draw conclusions and make evaluations—but not necessarily within the context of the real world. Proficiency in mathematics means being able to solve problems by applying integrated procedural knowledge and conceptual understanding—but, again, not necessarily real-world problems

I have never met a child without genius, but I have met children who come to my classroom feeling discouraged by past teachers who have focused on failure rather than growth.

connected to the experiences of children, particularly diverse children. What this data tells me is that the educational system is building mostly basic levels of understanding, not proficient or advanced. It also reminds me of *the data we still fail to collect*—such as equity data on identity, consciousness, or joy. We are not fully capturing the genius of students.

In the same year, the data showed that just 17 percent of Black fourth graders were proficient or advanced in reading and 15 percent in math. If those percentages are true, the nation should be outraged. But instead, we have people fighting to create laws and policies that prohibit the teaching of Black identity and Black justice in schools. *Do those people fail to see Black children as their own children?* If we are one nation, why aren't we all seeing the 17 percent and 15 percent as our own humanity?

There needs to be a dismantling of systems and curricula, and a (re)building of them that is grounded in the genius of our teachers and our students.

The othering of children still exists. Perhaps if those people viewed Black children as a part of their own people, maybe their laws and policies would uphold love, compassion, and anti-racism, rather than erasure.

The NAEP data also begs the question, do we have 17 percent reading proficiency of Black children, or do we have an educational system and literacy curriculum that responds to only 17 percent of Black children? Which one needs the "intervention" or "remediation," *the child or the system*? Which one needs reparations? I argue that traditional intervention and remediation have never widely helped children, especially those whose people have oppressive histories, because it is not the child who needs the intervention or remediation. It is the system and the curriculum that needs reparations. There needs to be a dismantling of systems and curricula, and a (re)building of them that is grounded in the genius of our teachers and our students. We only (re)build when we look back and (re)member history.

In *Cultivating Genius*, I asked, *how do we use the genius of the past to better educate the children of today?* I focused on the intellectual feasts and strivings of members of Black literary societies that gave us a guide—a road map—to improving education today. Members of those societies awakened and activated genius already inside of them. They used the word *genius* to name themselves in a world that didn't recognize their brilliance, purpose, or gifts.

In *Cultivating Genius*, I outlined four pursuits in education that moved beyond teaching skills only—skills disconnected from students' identities and world. I used *pursuit*, a word derived directly from African American ancestors, to denote the self-driven, purposeful practices designed to elevate children and humanity. I intentionally did not use *standard* because a standard is created by others and limits learning. Standards have a ceiling or stopping point, while pursuits continue throughout one's life.

1. **Identity Development:** Helping students to make sense of who they are and to learn about diverse cultural lives and identities of others.

2. **Skills Development:** Helping students to develop proficiencies across the content areas and state learning standards.

3. **Intellectual Development:** Helping students to gain new knowledge that connects to the context of the world where they can apply the skills and standards.

4. **Criticality Development:** Helping students to name, understand, question, and disrupt oppression (hurt, pain, and harm) in the world and within the self, and to work to make the world a better place.

These pursuits invite us to teach beyond traditional textbooks and worksheets alone, or teaching that is rote, prescriptive, and purely standardized test-driven. They enable students to see purpose and authentic meaning in their lives—past, present, and future. Once students begin to understand their purpose, they see the skills they learn as meaningful in the real world. Collectively, the pursuits are a new vision in education that name all content areas—not just social studies and English language arts—as humanities. This model invites us all to teach and learn with the goal of seeing the norm of our work as humanities. This means that within each classroom, we ask, *How can our content areas help children grow to be more humane and contribute to the earth?*

Introducing Joy!

In *Unearthing Joy*, I build upon the model in *Cultivating Genius* by adding the pursuit of *joy*—helping students to uplift beauty, aesthetics, truth, ease, wonder, wellness, solutions to the problems of the world, and personal fulfillment. Joy is the ultimate goal of teaching and learning, not test prep or graduation. Before writing *Cultivating Genius*, I assumed all educators, teachers, and administrators were building up to joy in their practices. In 2020, in the midst of a global pandemic and racial uprising, and the failure by many leaders to recognize the strength and pain of teachers and children, I realized that we needed joy more than ever. At the same time, with certain pressures on hold temporarily, educators started (re)claiming the joy and beauty of their pedagogy. They started to explore their creative sensibilities and bring more joy into the virtual classroom. We only

Joy is the ultimate goal of teaching and learning, not test prep or graduation.

get to learning and experiencing joy when we have an intentional and authentic purpose to dismantle oppression (again hurt, pain, or harm) in the classroom through criticality.

In *Unearthing Joy*, I also provide educators and those involved in teaching, learning, and leading the processes and tools for cultivating genius and joy. I call the book a "guide to teaching and learning" to address education through multiple spaces and realms in our lives, especially PreK–12 and higher education. My goal is to put history and theory into action in classroom practices that are exhilarating for students, parents, educators, and all those working for diversity, equity, and inclusion.

I don't think it's by chance that the word *human* is rooted in the Latin word *humus*, which means earth or ground. There is a connection between humanity and the growth of the earth. To engage in humanizing practices, we must return to the earth, return to the land.

We must unearth.

To unearth means to dig into the ground and bring excellence to light—to the sun. Unearthing requires digging, mining, and uprooting, and, ultimately, bringing genius to the surface—again, to the sun, revealing what has been pushed down and concealed. We must draw forth pedagogies of equity and excellence, moving students toward *the sun* (where they belong)—moving students and educators to genius and joy. The prefix of *un-* means to reverse, and I argue in this book that there is much in education to reverse.

Just as flowers are beautiful, children are genius. We don't give a flower its beauty. It is beautiful because that's its nature. In much the same way, we don't give children their genius. It is already there. Like flowers, children are destined for beauty and growth. They are the flowers. When a flower does not grow, we don't uproot it. Instead, we change the amount of sunlight and water, we change the type of soil, we nourish it. We look for solutions that will facilitate its growth. However, we teach Black children today in ways that uproot them from their histories and lineages, and from Black studies. The ways Black ancestors practiced math, science, and literacy are not used to teach Black children today. And then when they don't "grow," as they are destined to do, folks wonder why—and often begin to blame and punish others. Yet, when students do not "grow," it is because their roots have been removed from the rich soil of their existence. They have been deprived of the sunlight they need to bloom. If systems, structures, and practices were developed with the genius of diverse children in mind, we would see immense growth.

We have been watering some children's futures and not others. Can you imagine if the sun shined only on some of our children and not others? To say that only some students are genius implies the sun shines only for them. In our educational system, we dangerously plan for some students to succeed—*to see the sun*—and others to fail. We have given attention, care, and nurturing to some children and neglected others. But the sun is too massive and ubiquitous to say that some students should not be centered and honored in learning. The growth of a "flower" calls for work from the educator—the one who is nurturing the flower to grow. It calls for us to cultivate—which is a social action and responsibility. We are the ones who care for the flowers. We are the ones who water their genius.

Advancing the state of humanity, moving toward cultivation, calls for what Stevie Wonder sings about as "the promises of rain."

The rain, the water, the water to the earth.

But how can we water an earth that systemic racism and oppression have made dry?

This is the question that motivated me to write this book—and led to other questions that I asked myself as I wrote:

- *What does the water look like?*
- *How is water the joy for the barren lands of education?*
- *Why has our educational system remained dry—unchanged—for so long?*
- *How do we dismantle and reconstruct centuries of practices that have not served all children well, that have destroyed the futures of youth, especially Black, Brown, and Indigenous children—practices that allow only some students to see the sun and not others?*
- *Why are some textbooks so dry and disengaging?*
- *How do we cultivate not only the genius of students and educators, but also their joy?*
- *How do we begin to unearth and teach to the humanity of students and to the sustainability of the world?*
- *How can watering and unearthing be symbolic in the pursuit for creating an educational system—serving to disrupt harm and build a society that feels more human?*
- *How can we create systems, structures, and processes to ensure the growth of those we have failed the most in this country?*

The growth of a "flower" calls for work from the educator— the one who is nurturing the flower to grow. It calls for us to cultivate—which is a social action and responsibility.

The water is a special part of *Unearthing Joy*. In assuming the role of the waterer, we must recognize that water can be not only beneficial and helpful but also destructive and violent. We must be careful about the amount we use to water the genius of children. We must water to restore systems, schools, and classrooms.

Water has always played a special role in my life. I have a mother who believes a lack of water is the reason for any problem—ever. *If I had a bad day, if I tripped and fell, or if I simply didn't remember something, she told me I hadn't drunk enough water and if I had, those things certainly would not have happened.* Water nourishes. Also, when it rains, I always feel a new day is coming—a new beginning. Water renews. If we take the symbolic meaning of water across cultures, we learn that water is life-giving, and provides clarity and refreshment. Water is fertile.

When it rains, I always feel a new day is coming— a new beginning. Water renews.

I am reminded of the importance water had to Black and Indigenous ancestors. For example, in "The Negro Speaks of Rivers," Langston Hughes connects the natural flow of water to the growth and connections of various civilizations throughout history: "My soul has grown deep like the rivers," interrupting the misconception of Blackness as a monolith. In his writing, he describes the omnipresence of Blackness, moving across humanity and civilizations. Anna Julia Cooper connected water to the work of our ancestors as they "watered the soil" and to her identity as a Black woman, in *A Voice from the South*:

> I speak for the colored women of the South, because it is there that the millions of blacks in this country have watered the soil with blood and tears, and it is there too that the colored woman of America has made her characteristic history and there her destiny is evolving.

Black women have represented the water of culturally responsive education and have given us the model of how to advance curriculum, instruction, and leadership.

It is the water that makes us evolve. Bearing resemblance to Hughes and Cooper, in *Darkwater: Voices from Within the Veil*, W. E. B. Du Bois (1920) lifts the darker race by truth-telling about oppressive harms in the world, through carefully crafted essays on race and justice. He speaks of the "promises of rain" and education by stressing the need to unearth genius and joy, such as in this passage:

> Especially do I believe in the Negro Race: in the beauty of its genius, the sweetness of its soul, and its strength in that meekness which shall yet inherit this turbulent earth.
>
> I believe in the Training of Children, black even as white; the leading out of little souls into green pastures and beside the still waters, not for pelf

or peace, but for life lit by some large vision of beauty and goodness and truth…. (pp. 1–2).

Du Bois calls attention to the problems inflicting the earth and those we have neglected—and encourages us to view Blackness as a model and way forward for our children. Similarly, in examples of Indigenous cultures, water has signified strength, change, healing, and love (Dunbar-Ortiz, Mendoza, & Reese, 2019; Gilio-Whitaker, 2019). Water can be promise.

A Call for Humanizing Pedagogies

We need humanizing pedagogies that center the genius, justice, joy, love, and humanity of our children. That means we must *search for and unearth ourselves* and search for people, places, things, histories, movements, events, and moments that we have failed to teach because we didn't learn them ourselves. We can no longer have *hidden figures*. We must uncover them because we need their genius and their narratives to make us all better. The stories we teach matter, and in this book, I outline how we get to the genius and joy through curricular art and curricular stories of teaching and learning.

We can no longer have hidden figures. We must uncover them because we need their genius and their narratives to make us all better.

Drawing upon the gifts that ancestors and artists have given to the earth, I view the educator as the waterer—the cultivator—the *unearther*—the artist—the sculptor—the innovator—the songwriter—the storyteller—the designer of curriculum. I take educators (teachers, leaders, and other curriculum developers) through the practice of *unearthing*. When one unearths genius and joy, one creates a legacy by imprinting into the minds and hearts of children.

Chapter 1: *Unearthing the Need for Genius and Joy* In this chapter, I outline both the historical triumphs and the problems of systemic structures that have led us to education as we see it today. To understand education, we must study the history and the lingering effects it has. Specifically, I look at the roots and intersecting parts of a problematic system to justify the need to cultivate genius and unearth joy. I question why problems of the past continue today and call for new policies and practices to replace those in need of replanting. I lay out culturally and historically responsive education as a way forward.

Chapter 2: *Coming Into Joy* In this chapter, I focus on the pursuit of joy through the culturally and historically responsive education model (CHRE Model) for teaching and learning. I define *joy* and the process of unearthing it in schools and classrooms. I unpack each of the pursuits of CHRE Model—identity, skills, intellect, criticality, and joy—with rich examples of how they show up in learning across grade levels and content areas. Additionally, I answer frequently asked questions about the pursuits to build your understanding of how to implement the model.

Chapter 3: *Unearthing Self* In this chapter, I suggest that the starting point of culturally and historically responsive education is centering the self and doing the self-work. Educators cannot move to the pursuits of teaching identity, skills, intellectualism, criticality, or joy if they have not reflected upon and practiced the pursuits in their own lives. This chapter offers tools to do that work, while focusing on how to work with colleagues, parents, and community members who both support and resist culturally and historically responsive education.

Chapter 4: *Redesigning Curriculum and Assessment* In this chapter, I focus on how to design and implement instruction, and take you through a creative, step-by-step process. I include a set of practices and questions for guidance. I center the teacher as the artistic genius who creates meaningful and authentic learning experiences tailored to unique groups of students. In addition, I include tools for collecting equity data that go beyond traditional assessments for measuring children's reading or math levels alone. It is my hope that you will learn to collect data related to identity, skills, intellect, criticality, and joy. I write about effective practices of CHRE assessment and help educators learn ways to review and evaluate school curriculum for the CHRE pursuits.

A Note on "CRE," "CHRE," and the HILL Model

Throughout *Unearthing Joy*, I use "CRE" to denote culturally relevant or responsive education. With "CHRE" (culturally and historically responsive education), I build upon CRE by taking the past into consideration, emphasizing people and events that have traditionally been ignored or misrepresented in schools.

The HILL Model is my instructional framework for CHRE, in which I name the five pursuits—identity, skills, intellect, criticality, and joy—because they respond to diverse students' **H**istories, **I**dentities, **L**iteracies, and **L**iberation.

Chapters 5 and 6: *Practical and Creative Uses of the HILL Model* In these chapters, I provide practical applications of the CHRE Model across grade levels and content areas. I show how to teach the five pursuits through read-alouds, lessons and units, and literacy strategies, and to promote them through leadership approaches, family- and community-engagement strategies, and more. These applications showcase everyone involved in the system: students, teachers across the content areas, leaders, non-instructional staff, and parents, caregivers, and communities.

Chapter 7: *Planting Seeds for the Future* I conclude *Unearthing Joy* by highlighting the genius and joy of wonderful teachers across the world, who have not waited for or relied on anyone to provide what children have needed—teachers who have brought forth their excellence to ensure that children pursue identity, skills, intellect, criticality, and joy. In the last three years, they have created spaces of joy on social media by sharing ideas, questioning practices, and pointing us to a new way forward. They are models of the "promises of rain."

What You'll Find Across Chapters

The chapters build upon one another and, collectively, provide a guide for developing and revising CHRE curriculum and instruction. My hope is that each chapter feels like "tracks" in a symphony of word, poetry, and art on the page. If curriculum is the stories we teach and tell, this book helps you to name and justify which "stories" are worthwhile, while highlighting examples from schools. Instruction is how we share, experience, learn, and teach the stories. Often, we understand theoretically the need for equity and justice, but struggle with what it looks like in practice or where to begin. *Unearthing Joy* is a guide toward genius curriculum and instruction. I hope reading it is a multimodal experience of learning, reflection, and (re)membering.

My hope is that each chapter feels like "tracks" in a symphony of word, poetry, and art on the page.

The chapters begin with a set of "Unearthing Thought" questions that can be used for book clubs, literary societies, or self-reflection. Throughout chapters, I sprinkle in primary source documents to support my ideas because I appreciate the clarity that history offers. Each chapter is layered with art, poetry, music, and other textual content to elevate meaning, reflection, and joy. It also contains artwork, a musical playlist, and spaces for writing, coloring, and drawing out your own takeaways and meanings. My intention is for you to listen to the songs on the playlists (perhaps softly in the background) while reading, to heighten your understanding and joy. You may want to consider studying and discussing the songs' lyrics with colleagues, through the lens of teaching and learning. This intertextuality also helps with theoretical and practical learning. Readers may choose to study the meanings of the lyrics and connect the lyrics to the meanings held within the book. This book is intended to be read with ease, while provoking deep thought.

In addition to playlists of songs, I include a coloring page at the end of this introduction and each chapter to give you a purpose to pause and breathe for calm and joy. Coloring helps to connect the mind and heart, while returning us to childlike play and imagination. I suggest using colored pencils or fine-tip markers. (When using markers or pens on these pages, allow time for the ink to dry before touching the page or closing the book.)

I hope you leave *Unearthing Joy* with a greater sense of lessons, units, assessments, and other practical tools that you can use immediately with students—whether you teach young children; elementary, middle, or high school students; or adult learners or preservice teachers in formal or informal settings. I hope you feel me speaking to you as your partner in education—or as if we're two colleagues in conversation about the need for joy and justice in teaching and learning.

I write autobiographically throughout the book, sharing years of listening to people and being in awe of the earth. You may notice at times that I use the collective pronoun, *we*, because I don't do this work alone. I do it in the spirit of so many ancestors, children, teachers, and guides of the past, present, and future. My approach is inspired by an African philosophy called the *zamani* dimension, which means space of being and presence that is unconsciously, intuitively, or spiritually influenced by epistemologies and teachings of ancestral genius. It is my hope that readers today will become the ancestral legacies of the future.

I asked Pharrell Williams to open the book because so many of us are inspired by his artistry—by the way he pushes his genius across boundaries and the cosmos. When I first met Pharrell through his music, I found the five pursuits. I found elements of identity, a high level of skill, intellectualism, criticality and consciousness, and joy. When I observed Pharrell listen to his music, he closed his eyes as if he were experiencing joy—perhaps embodying the full earth of his artistry. It was beautiful. The way he looked when he created music is the way I look when I create curriculum. We are kindred souls in our artistry. It was a special gift for Pharrell to write the opening of this book—a text that is grounded in education as an art form.

I end the book much how I begin it, with the musical and theoretical musing of Stevie Wonder because he has offered genius and joy to help us all become better educators. He is certainly a gift to the earth. It is my splendid hope that *Unearthing Joy* is yet another gift to the earth.

I end this introduction by (re)membering and (re)visiting the words of Alice Walker:

> **The Nature of This Flower Is to Bloom**
> Rebellious. Living.
> Against the Elemental Crush.
> A Song of Color
> Blooming
> For Deserving Eyes.
> Blooming Gloriously
> For its Self.
> *Revolutionary Petunia.*

Our students are flowers who desire natural growth and the promises of the rain. They seek a rebellious bloom against control, authority, and convention that have not served them well, nor prepared them for the world—and the "elemental crush" of society that has not always centered their genius, and has instead focused on what they are not, or what they can't do. Yet, they grow and desire environments that nurture their growth.

Our students are a *Song of Color* and beauty. They are "Blooming," but only for those of "deserving eyes"—those who deserve to be in the presence of their greatness. Not every educator will deserve the privilege of teaching the next generation of leaders. But it is with hope that we prepare ourselves to do so.

Alice Walker states that the flower blooms gloriously for itself. The purpose of education is not to win prizes or to compete with others. It is not for one community to have more than another. The purpose of education is not to bolster our egos, but to ensure that students feel self-empowered, self-reliant, self-determined, and self-liberated. Education is for our students, not us. It is essential to center their voices, genius, and perspectives. For they are the "revolutionary petunias" or perhaps the "black orchids" who thrive vigorously, "gloriously," and vividly on the landscape of the beautiful earth. It is this harvest that will yield an education that is celebratory.

All I want to do is listen to the rain and watch the flowers grow.

—GHOLDY MUHAMMAD

Reflection

Select one or more questions to engage in a freewrite.

- **What are some reactions and reflections you have about the music, art, and text from this introduction?**
- **What ideas and passages stand out for you and why?**
- **What parts do you want to explore and learn about more?**
- **What parts of the educational system have helped you to grow?**
- **What parts of the educational system are in need of water?**
- **What do you plan to do to unearth genius and joy?**

Take some time to color this image.

Unearthing Joy: A Guide to Culturally and Historically Responsive Teaching and Learning

PART I

Tilling the Soil: Preparing Ourselves for Growth

CHAPTER 1

Unearthing the Need for Genius and Joy

"The world is a fine place and worth fighting for."

—ERNEST HEMINGWAY

LAYERED PLAYLIST

Songs that inspire me about genius and joy. Play them as you read this chapter.

"I Wish I Knew How It Would Feel to Be Free," Nina Simone

"Alabama," John Coltrane

"What's Going On," Marvin Gaye

"Let Up," Abbey Lincoln

"State of the World," Janet Jackson

"Gimme Mine," Tall Black Guy featuring 80s Babies

"Conversation Peace," Stevie Wonder

"If I Ruled the World (Imagine That)," Nas featuring Lauryn Hill

"I Shall Be Released," Nina Simone

"Blowin' in the Wind," Bob Dylan

Oppression
by Langston Hughes

Now dreams
Are not available
To the dreamers,
Nor songs
To the singers.

In some lands
Dark night
And cold steel
Prevail—
But the dream
Will come back,
And the song
Break
Its jail.

Freedom
by Langston Hughes

Freedom will not come
Today, this year
    Nor ever
Through compromise and fear.

I have as much right
As the other fellow has
    To stand
On my two feet
And own the land.

I tire so of hearing people say,
Let things take their course.
Tomorrow is another day.
I do not need my freedom when I'm dead.
I cannot live on tomorrow's bread.
    Freedom
    Is a strong seed
    Planted
    In a great need.
    I live here, too.
    I want my freedom
    Just as you.

Unearthing Thought

1. What type of PreK–12 education have you experienced? Whose cultures, stories, and histories were taught and represented? Whose were not? What type of learning did you experience or not experience?

2. What were problems from your own education? Do you still see those problems in schools today?

3. What examples of genius from your childhood helped you to learn and experience joy? Do you still see those examples in schools today?

4. If you could offer a metaphor for the educational system, what would it be and why?

5. What theories and models prepared you to be a teacher or leader? Are there theories and models that you still need? What are they?

6. Equity, justice, and culturally responsive practices have been around throughout history but have never been mandated in schools. Why do you think that is?

7. What is needed for equity, justice, and culturally responsive practices to be adopted and mandated in policy?

8. What are your thoughts when analyzing and critiquing these five parts of the system: 1) learning standards; 2) curriculum; 3) assessment/standardized tests; 4) teacher and leader evaluations; and 5) teacher education programs? How do those parts capture, express, evaluate, and build genius and joy? How is there a lack of culturally and historically responsive education?

9. What historical triumphs have shaped the system?

10. Given your state, district, and board policies, what kind of advocacy is needed to advance the system?

But Where Shall I Begin?

In her biographical account, *My Name Is Phillis Wheatley: A Story of Slavery and Freedom* (2009), activist-poet-scholar Afua Cooper writes in the voice of our beloved Sister Phillis Wheatley. She questions her starting point in narrating the life and times of Wheatley: "But where shall I begin? With my despair or with my triumph? Do I start with my life as an African child? Or my sufferings on the slave ship? Shall I begin with describing the first time I wrote a complete poem and tell of the sweet joy that flowed through my body? No. I shall begin with what I see shimmering in front of me."

Wheatley was an activist, poet, and writer who spent her life working toward a better humanity for Black people and, consequently, for everyone. She wrote about the life and times of the day, about humanity, and about joy. She wrote to (re) imagine a world absent of hurt, pain, harm, and injustice. Wheatley established a tradition of writing about the earth and its need for watering, in her poem, *On Imagination* (1773):

Phillis Wheatley

> Though Winter frowns to Fancy's raptur'd eyes
> The fields may flourish, and gay scenes arise;
> The frozen deeps may break their iron bands,
> And bid their waters murmur o'er the sands.
> Fair Flora may resume her fragrant reign,
> And with her flow'ry riches deck the plain;
> Sylvanus may diffuse his honours round,
> And all the forest may with leaves be crown'd
> Show'rs may descend, and dews their gems disclose,
> And nectar sparkle on the blooming rose.

In this glorious piece of writing, Wheatley allows us to visualize a world without enslavement or racism—and their harmful lingering effects. She (re)imagined a better, emancipated world, free of oppression, by detailing flourishing and fragrant landscapes blooming. It comes as no surprise why Cooper chose to study the life and writings of Wheatley. She opens her book by asking an important question: *Where should the story begin?*

Should the story begin with the despair and pain such as the suffering on the slave ship? Or shall her story begin with triumph and beauty, such as detailing her life as an African child where she was seen, heard, and loved? Cooper also ponders the thought of opening with "sweet joy" embodying the spirit of Wheatley's poetry writing.

I have been asking myself the same question as I open this book. Where should I begin the story of education—of children and of educators? Do I begin with despair, addressing the historic and oppressive structures that have created low achievement, low joy, low pay, and teachers leaving the field? Should I begin with the triumphs by addressing the beautiful genius that educators and children bring each day to schools? Or perhaps with joy? My inquiry was not a simple one, but it grabbed my attention because all three—despair, triumph, and joy—tell the truthful and complete narrative of education.

Despair is the result of structures and policies that have not always served children and teachers well. It is felt by teachers when they are intellectually trapped in curriculum that promotes low-level skills and contains texts that stifle their creativity. Much is also true of youth. Sometimes I wonder why we maintain such basic educational standards and models of mediocrity, given our brilliant history of people of color and other abolitionists, and the examples they provide. While some educators believe they are shifting the landscape, I wonder if their work is truly transformative. As a literacy teacher and scholar, I have witnessed new terms and titles for literacy programs, year after year. New terms and titles, however, do not mean different core approaches to literacies. Nor do they truly speak to transformation.

I also struggle with the fact that harmful structures of the past are still in place today, failing many children and teachers of color, especially Indigenous and Black children and teachers. Even districts with large percentages of children and teachers of color adopt models, evaluations, and frameworks that are not written by or designed for people of color. Rather, they are written by organizations, companies, and groups that don't reflect the identities and lives of the people for whom the materials are created.

Traditionally, schools share so-called equity data that narrates what children cannot do instead of what they can do. That data then becomes a prominent "story" of the school community. School leaders have even used data to create harmful programs and practices for students.

Defining Equity

Many approaches and programs in schools certainly do not offer students of color an opportunity for true or full equity. Equity has been mis-defined as simply providing rigor or access to all. But it is much more than that. Equity is teaching and learning that is centered on justice, liberation, truth, and freedom, and is free of bias and favoritism. You cannot talk about true justice, liberation, truth, and freedom without talking about anti-racism. Equity is not just about adding a multicultural book to the classroom library or providing access to something educationally good or sound. Doing that does not ensure that children will learn about their identities and histories, nor the liberation of themselves and others. Multicultural books can still be used to teach in incomplete and deficit ways. If a school has skills-only curriculum, and it reports only data from one skills-only standardized assessment, it isn't fully equitable. A school that is truly equitable embraces fairness and inclusion, and it responds to students' individual needs, providing structures, systems, and practices that enable all students to reach their highest potential for personal and academic success. Equity as access only, without addressing structural oppression/racism, isn't equity in its fullness. Schools that report only on test scores and gaps tell a false story rather than the truth of what led to those scores and gaps.

Given that, it is also fair to say that, too often, we do not tell stories of triumph, such as the stories of teachers who show up every day, striving for a holistic and complete education for their students, regardless of the limitations of standards, curriculum, or society. We also do not tell the stories of triumphs of children who are victorious despite being immersed in a system that is not designed to embrace their histories, identities, literacies, or liberation.

We certainly hardly ever begin the story with joy—joy of children, teachers, or leaders. During the COVID-19 pandemic, many individuals and organizations promoted the language of "learning loss." I deeply believe that there has been learning loss since the inception of public schools in the United States, given what was present and what was not. During the pandemic, learning loss did not feel new for children or teachers of color because of the historically countless missed opportunities to teach children who they are and whose they are. Companies yet again profited from sensationalized language. Yet no one really spoke of "joy loss." No one spoke of how joy is at the center of how we move in the world of education and why we return to school each day. In this chapter's opening excerpt about Phillis Wheatley, Cooper adds, I *shall begin* [the story] *with what I see shimmering in front of me*. I asked myself, *what is shimmering in front of us?*

I answered: Genius and joy. The genius and joy of our children and educators.

> *Equity is teaching and learning that is centered on justice, liberation, truth, and freedom.*

The story of schools rarely starts with genius and joy, and the ways liberatory educators have disrupted harmful learning. Joy is the beauty of learning that traditional state testing does not capture. Regardless of painful and misaligned educational practices, past and present, the genius and joy of our children still shimmer. We must (re)member the past and leaders such as Phillis Wheatley who give us examples of shimmering genius and joy.

A Brief History of Genius, Justice, and Joy

There are so many examples of genius, justice, and joy through history, which provide a great opportunity to learn from communities of color. Because I offer only a few in this section, I encourage you to seek more moments of and movements in genius, justice, and joy throughout history and today.

Beginning from ancient times of Timbuktu, Mali (West Africa), Black people carried gleaming genius.

The people of Timbuktu viewed literacy and books as treasures and road maps to discovering cultures and the global universe—and they protected, sustained, and elevated them. They made more wealth from the sale of books and manuscripts than from any other product (Saad, 2010). This is special, and a beautiful goal for today. Can you imagine if our nation's wealth came primarily from the sale of books? Their books were in demand and beautifully made from fine paper and ink. This is genius and joy. Their topics included Islam, mathematics, and science (Singleton, 2004). Books provided joy, personal fulfillment, and a pathway to freedom. When colonizers tried to seize their books—their sources of knowledge—for control and profit, the people of Timbuktu hid and protected them. That is genius. The lessons from this land and its people show how we must center genius, libraries, and diverse texts, and protect truth in knowledge.

In examples of shimmering genius and joy across the world, I am reminded of a time during 1800s enslavement, one of the most oppressive times in society, when the ancestors created genius through literacy/education. Literacy/education was the centering of the practices and livelihoods of African people. They always created a space when one did not exist. For example, to communicate routes to freedom, we would braid maps into young women and girls' hair. As such, hair braiding is not just beautiful and creative, but also connected to justice and liberation. Speaking to that, and to the genius of enslaved Africans, Ziomara

Books made by the people of Timbuktu

Asprilla García explained in a *Washington Post* article by DeNeen Brown that women would create "departes," thick, tight braids, with a bun at the top of their heads to send a message that they wanted to escape. "The curved braids would represent the roads they would use" (2011).

This history was not largely documented in print to protect Black people and enable them to continue to use hair braiding as a way to freedom.

Hair braiding to express higher levels of meaning and thinking also signified semiotics, mathematics, and geography before they became official disciplines of study in today's PreK–12 classrooms. Here lies a history embedded with identity, skills, intellect, criticality, and joy. The practice of literacies, geography, and STEM extended in reading the world through pathways, such as the Underground Railroad and Sister Harriet Tubman's reading of the night sky—the celestial gourd and the North Star, something natural and beautiful, as a map toward freedom (Dunbar, 2019). The ancestors read the earth as text and navigated themselves and others to freedom.

The ancestors also used what computer scientists now call *coding* and *algorithms* to send messages leading to freedom. They did that through music and lyrics. Songs contained coded messages. They were codified to signal protest and escape. It has been known that songs, such as "I Got My Ticket" and "Go Down Moses," were used as codes for fleeing to the North for safety. When the ancestors heard them sung, they knew they signified something prominent related to liberation. My youngest brother has a degree in computer science but, sadly, he was not offered a comprehensive history course that included this example. This would have been a great way to intro the history of coding and using codes for sending messages.

Go down, Moses
(Let my people go!)

Exodus VIII

Negro Spiritual
Arranged by
H. T. BURLEIGH

Voice

Piano

Is - rael was in E - gypt's lan' Let my peo-ple go, Op -

press'd so hard they could not stand, Let my peo-ple go.

(top) Hair braiding was used to communicate routes to freedom.

(bottom) Songs were codified to signal protest and escape.

This is yet another example of the genius of the times and a form of genius that we don't honor enough in schools.

The ancestors also embodied the gift of multiple literacies, such as Harriet Powers, who told stories of justice, joy, and truth in the literacy practice of quilting; not just speaking and writing. Too often, education privileges certain literacies. But children today have genius and, with it, multiple ways of showing meaning, just as they did in the past. Even when we ask children to take school, district, and state assessments, we do not ask them to showcase multiple literacies.

Genius was extended through creative, innovative, and expressive language practices, such as those of the Tutnese and Gullah Geechee people. Developed in the 18th century, Gullah is a creole language spoken by descendants of Africans in certain regions of South Carolina and Georgia (Geraty, 1997). It is derived from African languages, but mixed with forms of English—the language that was forced upon Africans to colonize them. Similarly, genius ancestors from Southern

Harriet Powers told stories of justice, joy, and truth in the literacy practice of quilting.

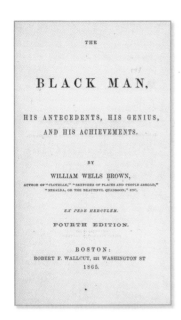

THE

BLACK MAN,

HIS ANTECEDENTS, HIS GENIUS,
AND HIS ACHIEVEMENTS.

BY

WILLIAM WELLS BROWN,

AUTHOR OF "CLOTELLE," "SKETCHES OF PLACES AND PEOPLE ABROAD,"
"MIRALDA, OR THE BEAUTIFUL QUADROON," ETC.

EX PEDE HERCULEN.

FOURTH EDITION.

BOSTON:
ROBERT F. WALLCUT, 221 WASHINGTON ST
1865.

regions also developed special and unique sounds and words that enabled them to communicate with one another. They called this language Tutnese or Tut language (McIlwain, 1995). Language devices were developed in secret because learning to read and write was forbidden. To create and develop new language is innovative and certainly genius. Sadly, though, these histories are not taught in most schools. We should begin to think about their implications for English language arts and communication courses today.

In addition, the ancestors created and used language to write about our genius and joy, and even used the term *genius* in the titles of books. See example to the left.

They created model learning spaces such as hush harbors, literary societies, and anti-slavery and other abolitionist organizations—all examples of genius from the nineteenth century, and the genius and joy carried into the next two centuries, as well as with the emergence of African-centered schools, Freedom Schools of the 1960s, Kitchen Table Talks, hip-hop, and other creative and intellectual modes of education. Through it all, we retained joy, even when striving for justice.

In the following example from the February 11, 1837, issue of the *Weekly Advocate* newspaper, one of the first African American publications, we see the power of learning:

> **READING.** He that would be an intelligent person must be a reading person. By reading you may visit all countries, converse with the wise, good, and great, who have lived in any age or country, imbibe their very feelings and sentiments, and view every thing elegant in architecture, sculpture, and painting. By reading you may ascend to those remote regions where other spheres encircle other suns, where other stars illumine a new expanse of skies, and enkindle the most sublime emotions that can animate the human soul.
>
> Without being a reading person, your information must be limited, and of a local nature.

Here, literacy (reading) and education were connected to genius, intelligence, and joy. We find beautiful language here of what education offers. It offers the beauty and ascensions in the world with goals of "enkindling sublime emotions that can animate the human soul." This is joy.

Rather than opening stories with the historic genius of children, too many of us instead use deficit terms to describe them—labels that demean them (e.g., non-white, minority, disadvantaged) and unjustly categorize them (e.g., struggling, unmotivated, nonreaders, low achievers). I have stopped using the term "minorities" because even when people of color are in the majority, they are still referred to as "the minority." I don't like including the word *minor* to refer to any group of people. Such terms are debilitating, potentially causing mental injury to youth as they internalize those terms and, as such, see themselves as "less than." To combat this, we must first study histories, systems, and structures of education that have led us to where we are today and their lingering effects. From there, we move to ways to implement healthier models and strategies for students.

The Earth Is in Need of Water

In the last 20 years, I have had opportunities to work across communities in leadership, teaching, and advisory positions, bearing witness to the beauty and essence of so many people striving for a better education for children. It became clear that in their striving, educators and community members have been working in a parched system designed to exclude children of color and other children who have been marginalized—and to exclude their genius and joy. In the introduction to this book, I asked a pivotal question: *How can we water the earth that systemic racism and oppression have made dry?* To understand joy and the need for joy, we must first study the earth and the systems of education that have inhibited and erased it from schools and classrooms—from students and educators.

Throughout my career, I have recognized the need for culturally responsive teaching and learning, but the educational system itself has been in great conflict with it and absent of it. Even when people of color and conscious leaders are on school boards, and are superintendents and principals, we still see few CRE/CHRE (culturally responsive education/culturally and historically responsive education) mandates. Even though we have research and scholarship on CRE/CHRE stemming from the 19th century, we still don't observe its theories, models, and practices reflected in school policies. In fact, CRE/CHRE feels like an add-on—or option for schools to enact. Many schools add it to professional development, yet leave their curriculum, evaluations, learning standards, and testing norms unchanged. Teachers are then left to wonder how to implement what a professional development provider recommended when they are going to be evaluated on opposite/standardized practices.

For example, if we take the Danielson Framework for teaching, which many districts use for teacher evaluation, we would not observe any explicit CRE/CHRE language other than academic skills. In school districts, we continue to use frameworks that were not written by or for Black educators or children, nor other people of color.

A Brief History of Erasure of Genius, Justice, and Joy

That absence of representation isn't coincidental.

A Measuring Rod...

In the late 1800s, Mildred Lewis Rutherford authored a book that was published and supported by the United Daughters of the Confederacy (UDC): *A Measuring Rod to Test Text Books, and Reference Books in Schools, Colleges and Libraries* (1920). It was designed to inform educators and educational publishers about what should and shouldn't be included in teaching and learning in K–12 schools, libraries, and universities. It also outlined how to select textbooks and curriculum for U.S. public schools and higher education. In essence, Rutherford attempted to offer a guide or playbook for school committees and leaders who select textbooks and curriculum, and for publishing companies that create those products. As the excerpt on the following page illustrates, Rutherford makes numerous biased statements. She clearly did not want schools to center the genius of Black people.

Rutherford also called for educators to "reject the book that speaks to the slaveholder of the South as cruel and unjust to his slaves," implying that they should spread the message that white slaveholders were kind and loving. She didn't even have the knowledge to call African people by loving and truthful names, for the ancestors were not "slaves." They were doctors, teachers, humanitarians, and thought leaders. At this time, the UDC centered the education of women and girls foremost because women were children's first teachers, and members wanted women to raise their children—and for girls to one day raise their children—with indoctrinated beliefs that enslavement was positive. They also taught this hate and falsehood to women first because there weren't many male teachers during the time, and the women would in turn teach this to their students. Also, the UDC taught such false things about oppressors because they did not wish for their children to think negatively of their fathers, grandfathers, and great-grandfathers. Rather than use moments to teach their children about anti-racism and abolition, they instead chose to conceal and shield the truth from them. It was Rutherford's mission to erase historical truths and to make enslavement a positive experience in curriculum. She did not want children to feel, what researchers later named, *white guilt*.

I think about parents today who fear their children will feel guilty for the oppression and crimes afflicted by people who look like them from the past. Guilt is an interesting construct in society. Currently in many states, there are initiatives for teachers to avoid making white children feel *guilty* for the actions of white oppressors, past and present. I have never encountered a historically responsive teacher who has made children feel guilty for something they didn't do. *Do folks in society have affinity and connections to slaveholders and others who inflict harm, when they could have chosen love?* If so, maybe that is why they still work to create laws today—to enforce this continued hate for Black people and erasure of truth.

WARNING*†

Do not reject a text-book because it does not contain all that the South claims—a text-book cannot be a complete encyclopedia.

Do not reject a text book because it omits to mention your father, your grandfather, your personal friend, socially or politically—it would take volumes to contain all of the South's great men and their deeds.

Do not reject a text-book because it may disagree with your estimate of the South's great men, and the leaders of the South's Army and Navy—the world can never agree with any one person's estimate in all things.

But—reject a book that speaks of the Constitution other than a Compact between Sovereign States.

Reject a text-book that does not give the principles for which the South fought in 1861, and does not clearly outline the interferences with the rights guaranteed to the South by the Constitution, and which caused secession.

Reject a book that calls the Confederate soldier a traitor or rebel, and the war a rebellion.

Reject a book that says the South fought to hold her slaves.

Reject a book that speaks of the slaveholder of the South as cruel and unjust to his slaves.

Reject a text-book that glorifies Abraham Lincoln and villifies Jefferson Davis, unless a truthful cause can be found for such glorification and villification before 1865.

Reject a text-book that omits to tell of the South's heroes and their deeds when the North's heroes and their deeds are made prominent.

Refuse to adopt any text-book, or endorse any set of books, upon the promise of changes being made to omit the objectionable features.*

A list of books, condemned or commended by the Veterans, Sons of Veterans, and U. D. C., is being prepared by Miss Rutherford as a guide for Text-Book Committees and Librarians.

This list of course contains only the names of those books which have been submitted for examination. Others will be added and published monthly in *"The Confederate Veteran,"* Nashville, Tennessee.

* The endorsement of a series of Historical Novels, "The Real Romance of History," was once given by the Historian-General, U. D. C., upon the promise to change the objectionable statements regarding the War between the States. The endorsement was used but the promise was not kept—her endorsement sold many books containing the falsehoods.
† There was not time to submit this "Warning" to the Veterans or Sons of Veterans, but Miss Rutherford thinks it will meet with their approval.

5

Excerpt from *A Measuring Rod to Test Text Books, and Reference Books in Schools, Colleges and Libraries*

Audre Lorde (1984) offers some clarity on the matter, while evoking water and the earth:

> I have no creative use for guilt, yours or my own. Guilt is only another way of avoiding informed action, of buying time out of the pressing need to make clear choices, out of the approaching storm that can feed the earth as well as bend the trees (p. 121).

If any human inflicts harm, that human should feel guilty. That is a healthy emotional response. It is those who feel nothing who we should worry about. It is problematic and incorrect to believe that oppressors of the past did no harm, and that our children should not learn the truth behind oppressors' action—to think, *My children might see themselves in oppressors, and I don't want them to feel guilty*. This mentality does not advance humanity nor show any care for Black and Brown children. We should be asking, Why would children see themselves in racists or anyone who has harmed others? What are we avoiding here? According to Audre Lorde, we are avoiding justice-oriented actions. We are avoiding the earth's needed water.

Yet, we know *A Measuring Rod* was an example of how falsehood is indoctrinated in schools and communities. Rutherford's mission was largely successful. The textbooks that followed taught false and distorted depictions of American history and Black history (Loewen, 2014). What is unique also about *A Measuring Rod* is the absence of student voice. We do not hear children's views of lies and injustice. We do not hear their critiques of "slaveholders." We don't see the guide for white children to identify as abolitionists. We see only an agenda designed to harm children of color. And still, no one thought, *How would such an agenda for curriculum make children feel and love—or to be in the world?*

This erasure and denial of truth in history does not help children become conscious, empathic beings. Rather, the opposite can happen—students may not develop critical literacies that are necessary to question, challenge, and ultimately resist such fabrication. Without critical literacies, students may become passive producers and consumers of knowledge. And that can be dangerous, as children grow older and select friends and partners, make purchases, make medical decisions, and choose candidates to vote for. They may accept anything as truth so that even oppression feels like equity.

History has shown repeated examples of oppressors working to make injustice, violence, and inequities acceptable and appear like good things. Texts such as *A Measuring Rod* do not allow students to experience joy because students are continually lied to through pedagogy. Students need to see themselves in pedagogy and be told the truth to be joyful. In *A Measuring Rod*, Rutherford not only neglected to show the genius of Black people (1920), she called for textbooks to depict Black people as joyful only when enslaved. In another publication, she states, "The servants were very happy in their life upon the old plantations" (quoted in Case, 2002, p. 611). Here, for all intents and purposes, she glorifies concentration camps and connects benefits and even happiness to them. If the history of a people is steeped in the "happiness" that comes from being enslaved and violently killed, raped, and oppressed, what does it suggest about Blackness and history? How would Black students feel after receiving this kind of instruction? How would other students feel about Black classmates?

Teaching Black joy means teaching the truth about historical and current events, and especially the truth about the lives of people who have been oppressed in the past. Even when Black folks were fighting oppression through music and art, we had joy in our creativity and collectivism—joy that is largely untaught. The effects of *A Measuring Rod* continue to linger in schools. We still see falsehood and erasure of people of color's humanity today.

The New England Primer

The New England Primer was a children's textbook developed in the 1600s by British journalist Benjamin Harris, who emigrated to Boston, and is my second example of the erasure of genius, joy, and justice. The book followed Harris's earlier textbook, *The Protestant Tutor: Instructing Children to Spel and Read English, and Grounding Them in the True Protestant Religion and Discovering the Errors and Deceits of the Papists.* The primer was published widely throughout the United States and Europe, and, in fewer than 100 pages, became the foundation for the teaching and learning of reading and literacy. Primers of the day tended to be short, likely due to the expense of importing paper from England (Barry, 2008). *The New England Primer* was published in response to the Massachusetts law, the Old Deluder Satan Act of 1647, which mandated reading instruction for individuals to learn how to read print text along with the Bible. Learning to read through the Bible was common then for public education. The wording of "ye old deluder, Satan" meant "to keep one away from Satan" and toward the teachings of the Bible (Willis & Harris, 2000). The word *primer* originally referred to a book of prayers, so it likely comes as no

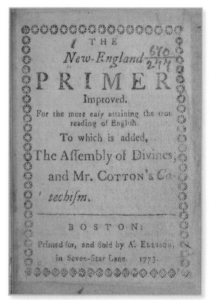

The New England Primer

Excerpt from *The New England Primer*

surprise to see how religion connected to this text. The Old Deluder Satan Act specifically required white communities to provide their children with literacy teachers.

The goal of *The New England Primer* was to teach and normalize white Christian culture. To the left is a page from it. You can probably see, through a Christian-centered lens, that children learned to read using rote memorization and rime schemes. You can also see that there are animals in the text, along with white males.

The primer extended the textual teachings of the *Hornbook*, which followed this sequence of instruction: recognizing letters of the alphabet, then letter sounds, then sound blends or syllables, which led to simple and complex sentences. The *Hornbook* was used by children for several centuries, beginning in the mid-15th century, in Europe and the United States. The *Hornbook* was actually not a book at all, but rather a wooden paddle with lessons engraved on it along with the alphabet and the Lord's Prayer, and a leather carrying strap.

No child benefits from seeing or learning about a single culture.

Compared to the *Hornbook*, *The New England Primer's* content was more religious in nature and addressed sin (Barry, 2008). It was also adapted into *The Indian Primer*, which propagated the same glorification of whiteness and racist, false views of Indigenous people. The Indian Primer, which, of course, was not authored by an Indigenous person, was intended to convert Native people to the primer's version of Christianity.

Problems With the Primer

The first enslaved Africans were violently forced to the United States in 1619, about 70 years before *The New England Primer* was published. The primer did not reflect authentic experiences and identities of children of color. We can infer that oppressors' children learned to read using the primer at school and home, and grew up teaching others the way in which they were taught. The problems related to *The New England Primer* are worth exploring today because the book established the foundation for education as we know it. So, next, I lay out the problems related to the primer, whose repercussions we are still dealing with in education today. Consequently, we have a deep need for CRE/CHRE models and practices to advance the achievement of youth moving forward.

Problem 1: The primer was centered on whiteness and white representation, including white characters and culture. It contained no diversity or people of color. It did not contain examples of Black excellence, Black thought, or Black ways of developing literacy. Therefore, it was anti-Black. The same can be said for the excellence and cultural ways of Indigenous people and other people of color. In fact, the text included more representations of animals than people of color. The hegemonic nature of the book prompts the question, *Who was represented and who was not?* It was ahistorical to the histories, identities, and educational needs of people of color. There is a myth that white children benefit when they only see themselves in curriculum. That is false and does a great disservice to white children. No child benefits from seeing or learning about a single culture. Children must see diverse representations of their own lives and of the lives of others, whose race, culture, and/or gender may be different from theirs.

This problem connects to research conducted by the University of Wisconsin-Madison (2019), which proves that there is still a lack of representation in books used in schools. If the curriculum (and books taught within curriculum) is like a mirror, it should reflect wide, varied, and beautiful manifestations of children's lives (Bishop, 1990). Often, educators don't feel the text alone is problematic because it connects to one of many identities of children. When I was a child, I loved The Baby-Sitters Club series and other books, in which I saw some of my identities, but certainly not all of them. The mirror must reflect multiculturalism and diverse identities.

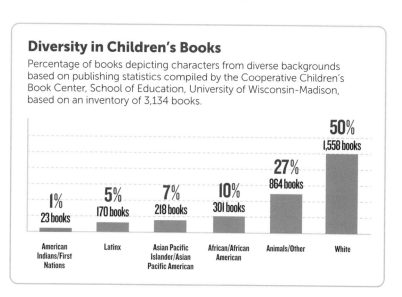

Diversity in Children's Books

Percentage of books depicting characters from diverse backgrounds based on publishing statistics compiled by the Cooperative Children's Book Center, School of Education, University of Wisconsin-Madison, based on an inventory of 3,134 books.

1% 23 books	5% 170 books	7% 218 books	10% 301 books	27% 864 books	50% 1,558 books
American Indians/First Nations	Latinx	Asian Pacific Islander/Asian Pacific American	African/African American	Animals/Other	White

Problem 2: The primer was apolitical and lacked criticality and social justice.
It did not acknowledge misrepresentations, racism, sexism, injustices, oppressions, social injuries, or social urgencies of the times. It did not offer opportunities for children to understand race, gender, class, sexuality, religions other than Christianity, or other forms of intersectionality. *Did we need social justice in the 1600s?* Of course we did—just as we need it today. The text was dysconscious and decontextualized with regard to critical problems in society, and, therefore, lacked diversity of thought. Children learning from the primer were not encouraged to think beyond the author's intent. Still today, we see much curriculum for early literacy/early readers with no criticality or examples of social justice.

Problem 3: The primer did not provide opportunities for all children to see themselves or to make sense of their multiple identities. Because of the primer's focus on whiteness, it appeared as if white people were the only people who mattered in society. Also, only two gender identities were represented and there were no opportunities for young people to see themselves, to define themselves, or to make sense of their lives and ideologies.

Problem 4: The primer privileged the English language. Although other languages were spoken during the 1600s, the primer featured only a specific type of English, and it was taught to Indigenous children whose home/cultural language was not English. Despite the fact that there are a growing number of languages spoken in the United States (NCTE, 2020), those languages are still not largely used, nor represented, in curriculum, assessments, state tests, and textbooks.

Problem 5: The primer promoted skills only and did not explicitly offer opportunities for cultivating the pursuits of identity, intellectualism, criticality, and joy. The meaning on each page was solely held within the author's intention and not the individual reader's interpretation. Identity and criticality bring the readers' identities and critical interpretations to the meanings. Furthermore, there were no opportunities to interrogate or debate the text, or respond in writing to it. Skills-only instruction usually involves only textbooks, worksheets, and lectures. We don't see much innovation when curriculum is decontextualized from global lives or identities.

Implications for Education Today

These problems from the early 1600s are still present in structures and mandates of schools today, particularly when it comes to the following five central parts of education:

1. Teaching and Learning Standards and Policies
2. Curriculum and Instruction
3. Assessments and State Tests
4. Teacher and Leader Evaluations
5. Teacher Education Programs

These parts of education impact the outcomes of children and types of children we seek to develop in our schools, but it is possible to still revise them to be more culturally and historically responsive. If we use the power we hold to change any of these parts, we will see a different educational system. We will see joy.

Unearthing Teaching and Learning Standards and Policies

Commonly, state standards are written to address only one-fifth of the culturally and historically responsive model: skills. They do not consider identity, intellect, criticality, and joy. And too often, they lack rigor and excellence. For example, to meet the 2022 Georgia Standards of Excellence (revised last in 2016 to date), kindergartners learn the following social studies skills and content—specifically, according to the standards, "the foundations of the social studies strands…. United States history through the study of important American holidays and symbols."

Historical Understandings. SSKH1 Identify the national holidays and describe the people and/or events celebrated.

a. Christmas
b. Columbus Day
c. Independence Day
d. Labor Day
e. Martin Luther King, Jr. Day
f. Memorial Day
g. New Year's Day
h. Presidents Day (George Washington, Abraham Lincoln, and the current president)
i. Thanksgiving Day
j. Veterans Day

SSKH2 Identify the following American symbols:

a. The national and state flags (United States and Georgia flags)

b. Pledge of Allegiance

c. Star-Spangled Banner (identify as the national anthem)

d. The bald eagle

e. The Statue of Liberty

f. Lincoln Memorial (identify image and associate with Abraham Lincoln and Presidents Day)

g. Washington Monument (identify image and associate with George Washington and Presidents Day)

h. White House (identify image and associate with Presidents Day and the current president)

What do you notice about these standards?

When reading these standards, I thought about what is missing. There is no mention of women, people of color, multiple-language speakers, or white abolitionists. If we are going to teach about those who have inflicted harm on others, we must tell children the truth, or they may grow older needing to unlearn what they've been taught. According to SSKH2, it's more important to teach about the bald eagle than people of color, and how can one teach "foundations" without acknowledging Indigenous people? This list does not suggest "excellence" in learning, as the name of the standards implies.

I argue that we either need a new set of learning standards or a model to teach the existing standards more excellently.

Furthermore, the skills are very low level. To "identify" is not rigorous, even for this grade level—to "identify and critique" would be more rigorous. I argue that we either need a new set of learning standards or a model to teach the existing standards more excellently. A reframed list of standards would develop more than just the skills. It would also develop identity, intellect, criticality, and joy. New standards can be a part of any content or grade level that is more "common" to all children, not just Eurocentric histories. My hope is that we will not see similar standards for learning in years to come.

Until then, below I show how you might teach two of the substandards through a CHRE lens. I have added a family/home connection because we must not teach anything, and students must not learn anything, without our first partners in education: the child's family (however family is defined).

SSKH1 b. Columbus Day

This standard implies Christopher Columbus was a hero and did not inflict harm on others. Therefore, students should be given opportunities to critique the standard, and it should be modified.

Identity: Students will learn about the cultural genius of Indigenous peoples.

Skill: Students will identify, analyze, and critique Columbus Day.

Intellect: Students will learn about Indigenous Peoples' Day and its history.

Criticality: Students will learn about the importance of naming holidays that reflect truth, anti-oppression, and diversity.

Joy: Students will learn ways we can celebrate the beauty of Indigenous peoples and Indigenous Peoples' Day.

Family/Home Connection: As a family, who would we choose to name a holiday after (someone who has made the world or communities better for all)?

SSKH2 c. Star-Spangled Banner (identify as the national anthem)

This standard implies that "The Star-Spangled Banner" is the only national anthem, which is not true. For example, there is the Black national anthem, "Lift Every Voice and Sing," by John Rosamond Johnson and James Weldon Johnson.

Listen to "Lift Every Voice and Sing," Alicia Keys

Identity: Students will identify songs that give them self-pride.

Skill: Students will identify, analyze and critique "The Star-Spangled Banner."

Intellect: Students will learn about the history of "The Star-Spangled Banner" from the perspectives of people of color in the 19th century.

Criticality: Students will learn about the importance of language written to harm others and why people resisted the full song lyrics.

Joy: Students will learn about the song, "Lift Every Voice and Sing," and the beauty in it.

Family/Home Connection: As a family, make a playlist of songs that lifts our joy.

If the unit were taught according to the standard alone, imagine what children would not learn. In each of these examples, skills connect to something worthwhile in the world. If standards were taught as skills alone, students would miss out on content and opportunities to make connections. By reframing standards according to the five pursuits, as I've done here, we contextualize skills and give students ways to connect them to the real world and their lives. Doing that will not eliminate teaching in deficit or basic ways, but it will shrink the chances. Skills that are not explicitly connected to culture, race, identity, consciousness, or joy could lead to that kind of teaching--teaching that is detached from humanity. We must be watchful of that.

Standards should not be reserved only for students. They should be created for and extended to educators. In addition to the evaluations, educators need a set of standards—or pursuits, as the ancestors affectionately named them. Such pursuits will guide educators and hold them accountable for culturally and historically responsive teaching, learning, and leading. Consider the following pursuits as a start to creating more excellent, more responsible standards for students.

Identity: Teachers and leaders must learn about and show evidence of students' histories, identities, literacies, and liberation. They must authentically respond to students' identities in curriculum, instruction, and leadership practices.

Skills: Teachers and leaders must demonstrate proficient reading, writing, speaking/communication, and content or disciplinary skills, centered in critical love and cultural understandings.

Intellect: Teachers and leaders must exhibit knowledge of multiple cognitive, sociocultural, and critical theories, methods, and scholars/scholarship. They must show proficient or advanced knowledge of what it means to be a scholar of their discipline and profession, and exhibit varied and excellent methods of instruction and leadership.

Criticality: Teachers and leaders must exhibit knowledge and practice of consciousness, and critical thinking, teaching, and leading. They must understand how to name, understand, question, research, and disrupt oppression (hurt, pain, and harm of varied forms in humanity).

Joy: Teachers and leaders must understand how to connect beauty, aesthetics, wellness, wholeness, solutions to problems, and/or happiness to their curricular, instructional, and leadership practices.

When these pursuits are authentically woven into strategic plans (and not merely added as a "component" of those plans), we can then move to adoption of and mandates for policy.

Suggestions for Teaching and Learning Standards and Policies

- Revise state standards to include elements of identity, intellect, criticality, and joy.
- Adopt culturally and historically responsive learning standards for student learning.

- Adopt a model to teach current, unchanged standards in culturally historically responsive ways.
- Adopt culturally and historically responsive teaching and learning standards for teachers and instructional support staff, leaders, and board members.

Unearthing Curriculum and Instruction

Curriculum and instruction today are still mostly, if not only, skills-driven, absent of cultural and historical responsiveness. Curriculum is defined as anything we teach, and the instruction is *how* we teach the curriculum. The "how" we teach curriculum should be detailed in the full package teachers are provided. According to the New York University Metro Center, curriculum includes the "detailed package of learning goals; units and lessons that lay out what teachers teach each day and week; assignments, activities and projects given to students; and books, materials, videos, presentations, and readings used in the class" (2019). With that definition in mind, the curriculum can take the form of a basal reader, a textbook, or a packaged program typically purchased from a publishing company. However, many schools use checklists, syllabi, or a list of standards as their curriculum, which, alone, do not qualify as a full, high-quality curriculum. They serve best as the basis of curriculum to be written. National problems of curriculum include:

- The authors of the curriculum are unclear—including their background in teaching students of color.
- The curriculum lacks equity and culturally responsive education.
- The curriculum has multicultural concepts and some justice-oriented essential questions; yet users consider it fully culturally responsive.
- The curriculum lacks intricate multiculturalism and tokenizes culture.
- The curriculum is grounded in skills only, with no learning objectives or assessments for other pursuits of learning.
- The curriculum is difficult to navigate for teachers and students.
- The curriculum was developed without the input and agreement of young people.
- The curriculum does not reflect the histories, identities, literacies, or liberation of people of color.
- Principals do not understand the curriculum.
- Parents do not understand the curriculum.
- Students do not understand the curriculum.

- The curriculum has not historically responded to the personal and achievement needs of all students.
- The curriculum contains examples of Black or Indigenous history, but it is taught from the perspective of the colonizer.
- The curriculum does not capture the genius and joy of people of color.

Of course, the goal is to embrace humane curriculum and instruction, where students position skills learning in the context of the real world, urgent issues, and diverse people in society. We know that silencing the call for social justice can be dangerous and problematic because it puts children's humanity at stake.

Suggestions for Curriculum and Instruction

- Put out an RFP (request for proposal) to an organization to write a curriculum that you desire for your students.
- Create a rubric or other form of content document that curriculum writers at publishing companies follow, rather than their writing the curriculum without your input.
- Ask publishing companies to conduct random focus groups made up of your districts' children to test the curriculum's effectiveness before purchasing it.
- Consider funding teachers and partners to collaborate on writing or redesigning your school's curriculum.
- Redesign your curriculum according to the five pursuits: skills, identity, intellect, criticality, and joy.
- Organize more diverse content developers that include children, parents, community leaders, scholars, researchers, teachers, noninstructional staff, teachers, school administrators and others who have useful input.

Unearthing Assessments and State Tests

To assess means to gather information to determine how students are experiencing the learning and how well specific pursuits are being enacted in the classroom, school, or district. As educators, we are constantly gathering information from students to examine what we need to do next to inform our instruction or leadership. Yet, traditionally, that information is focused on skills—typically, students' reading and math levels. We rarely, if ever, collect data on identity, intellect, criticality, or joy. State tests have also held bias and lacked CRE/CHRE content, from characters' names in passages to the type of content we deem as important to know. State assessments (a billion-dollar, for-profit industry) center skills only. What if states collected more data along with test skills that they can triangulate with students' achievement levels? In other words, what if we compared progress within other pursuits to compare with their skill levels? What if we measured and collected data on the things we value? We must show we value more than skills. We must unearth new methods of data collection, research questions, and what we learn of our students. We must also provide state and large-scale assessment in multiple languages. It is sad that, even when English is not a child's first language, that child may still be required to be tested using English-only assessments. In Chapter 4, I offer practical ways to assess the five pursuits.

Suggestions for Assessment

- Create protocols and assessment tools to gather dialogistic, formative, summative, and criterion-referenced data across the five pursuits.
- Create ongoing large-scale assessments for parents, students, teachers, community members, leaders, and board members related to the five pursuits.
- Provide assessments in multiple languages.

Unearthing Teacher and Leader Evaluations

Teacher and leader evaluation is a key piece of the systemic puzzle and a key part of culturally and historically responsive education. If there are teachers or leaders who do not desire identity, skills, intellect, criticality, and joy for students, and don't want to teach and lead in this way (and aren't evaluated in this way), they know they don't *have* to change their practices. We have mandated skills teaching, but not the teaching of identity, intellect, criticality, or joy. We need to ask who wrote our district or city's teacher evaluation. Were they conscious educators who have taught Black and Brown children? Were they people of color? Were Black women on the committee? (Black women have experienced multiple forms of injustice and, therefore, have brilliant perspectives.) I find that in many urban districts, 85–89 percent of children of color adopt evaluations written by white women who never intended those evaluations to be used for culturally responsive education. We need alignment to CHRE standards, curriculum, and assessment. We can no longer afford to keep educators who either inflict explicit or implicit harm or do not keep up with the times. Education must be reserved for the brightest, most genius, and most conscious among us. This is also important for how we recruit and hire new educators.

Suggestions for Evaluation

- Consider what type of teacher or leader is desired and if the evaluation reflects that type.
- Interrogate the evaluation for explicit language around the five pursuits.
- Revise or rewrite evaluation to hold teachers and leaders accountable and responsible for culturally and historically responsive education.

Unearthing Teacher Education

As a professor and teacher educator, almost every day I deep dream about what the next generation of teachers needs to be well and to be successful. School leaders must reserve funding by going to area universities and demanding (to use the language of youth) the types of classes and other forms of professional development that are needed for candidates to be hired in their districts. As we strengthen school-university partnerships, how can we recruit and admit students into teaching programs based on different criteria? When speaking to music and art students, I noticed that many programs require a portfolio or audition. I considered a process to audition the potential genius of students who were called to education so that everyone isn't admitted into a teacher education program and that genius potential teachers are not excluded. I had an experience with a student who was admitted into a teaching program even though that student had written very racist things about Black people in an application essay. That student received top grades (even in a diversity course) and graduated with an education degree. To this day, I don't understand how someone who demeaned a group of people can then go out into the world to teach children who belong to the same group that the teacher demeaned. I wondered, what if we had unique requirements for this student to enter the teacher education program? What if he had to create a portfolio and artistic showcase of ideas that displayed his potential to teach excellence across Black cultures?

We must screen the genius and consciousness of those who will be teachers and give them an education that evaluates their minds, hearts, and responsiveness, and not just their ability to teach content skills. Additionally, we must ensure that teacher candidates are learning from diverse thinkers beyond Vygotsky, Dewey, Piaget, and Maslow. We don't typically see thinkers on the syllabus such as Mary McLeod Bethune, Carter G. Woodson, W. E. B. Du Bois, Anna Julia Cooper, Maria Stewart, Elizabeth Flood, or Clara Muhammad. Programs must not offer just one course in diversity, CRE, or consciousness. Instead, all courses must somehow honor this approach to learning.

Suggestions for Teacher Education

In my deep dreaming, a reframed teacher-education program would have the following courses:

- **Self and Humanity:** *a course devoted to discovery and unpacking of self, ideologies, social conditions and thinking, and how our own identities and histories affect teaching for humanity*

- **History of BIPOC Literacy Education:** *a course devoted to ways BIPOC have engaged in wide literacies to develop education across the disciplines across the globe*

- **Theories of Education:** *a course devoted to learning of multiple theories and how they help to explain methods, strategies, and current practices in education*

- **Becoming Scholars of Disciplines:** *a course devoted to learning how to observe the world in mathematics, science, social studies, and English language arts and how to authentically connect skills/standards to the world and needs for humanity*

- **CHRE core course and CHRE embedded in methods courses:** *a core course devoted to history and practical learning of culturally and historically responsive education and other resource models for learning, followed by subsequent practice of the five pursuits in methods courses*

- **Joy, Self-Care, and Wellness:** *a course devoted to ways educators can elicit and enact joy and wellness in their own lives, in the classroom, and at school*

Dismantling and (Re)building: Searching for Joy in the Gardens

> "We are a people. A people do not throw their geniuses away. And if they are thrown away, it is our duty as artists and as witnesses for the future to collect them again for the sake of our children."
>
> —ALICE WALKER, *In Search of Our Mothers' Gardens: Womanist Prose*

When these five parts of the system (standards/policies, curriculum, assessment, evaluation, and teacher education) are (re)built, we will see the potential for joy among children and educators. In this book, I aim to write for the human condition and provide the water (materials and tools) needed to (re)plant systems and the thinking to grow more evolved schools and classrooms—thereby reviving systemic structures of education. In education, there must be structural change for those inside of and affected by the system. The system and the people within it need (re)planting and the opportunity to grow, using materials and tools that have historically proven to be effective. Those already striving for humanizing practices need supports for sustainability.

If you are like me, you are tired of celebrating "despite students"—students who achieve despite a system that did not nurture or love them. I was a "despite student," one who did not see a teacher of color in high school or learn about the genius or joy of Black women. Yet, I achieved. I was celebrated. But imagine how children could excel when the system is designed for their full success—where they don't have to overcome the system or be someone else to thrive. As educators, or waterers, we can help children reach their genius—bloom to their greatness—through culturally and historically responsive pedagogies. In Chapter 2, I unearth curriculum further, providing ways for you to move toward the pursuit of joy, the ultimate goal for education.

Chapter 1 Reflection

Select one or more questions to engage in a freewrite.

- **What are some reactions and reflections you have about the music, art, and text from Chapter 1?**
- **What ideas and passages stand out for you and why?**
- **What parts do you want to explore and learn about more?**
- **What parts of the educational system have helped you to grow?**
- **What parts of the educational system are in need of water?**
- **What do you plan to do to unearth genius and joy?**

Take some time to color this image.

CHAPTER 2

Coming Into Joy

"We need Joy as we need air. We need Love as we need water. We need each other as we need the earth we share."

—MAYA ANGELOU

LAYERED PLAYLIST

Songs that inspire me about the importance of embracing joy. Play them as you read this chapter.

"Another Star," Stevie Wonder

"Be Alive," Beyoncé

"Don't Worry, Be Happy," Bobby McFerrin

"Break My Soul," Beyoncé

"Escapade," Janet Jackson

"I Got You (I Feel Good)," James Brown and The Famous Flames

"Happy," Pharrell Williams

"Shout, Pts. 1 & 2," The Isley Brothers

"Off the Wall," Michael Jackson

"Walking on Sunshine," Katrina and the Waves

Joy
by Langston Hughes

I went to look for Joy,

Slim, dancing Joy,

Gay, laughing Joy,

Bright-eyed Joy—

And I found her

Driving the butcher's cart

In the arms of the butcher boy!

Such company, such company,

As keeps this young nymph, Joy!

Unearthing Thought

1. How do you define joy?

2. What is an experience from your own PreK–12 education that brought you joy in learning? What did the teacher do or not do?

3. How (often) was joy centered in your teacher preparation, and now in your school or district?

4. How are your communities, schools, and classrooms absent of joy?

5. How are your communities, schools, and classrooms rich with joy?

6. In what ways do you observe joy in your curriculum (instruction and assessment)?

7. What do you believe is the purpose of curriculum?

8. How do your observations align with your beliefs about the purpose of curriculum?

9. What child do you hope your instruction and leadership will cultivate? What are the qualities and characteristics of that child? Will skills-only curriculum and instruction help you nurture that child?

10. How do you currently teach and lead for joy?

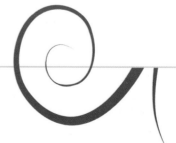

Strive to Feel Beauty, Wholeness, Wellness, and Happiness

When I was a child, I knew I would become a teacher. The profession was something I chose, but I also feel it chose me. Even when I took other career paths, my journey always wound up back on the teaching path. Teachers were my heroes. While some kids would look up to athletes and entertainers (who were special, too), I looked up to teachers. I wanted to dress like them, talk like them, and beautifully command presence like them. I watched their teacherly moves and wanted to emulate them. Teachers had power in the world, and I wanted some of that power to change the minds and hearts of others, and my own mind and heart.

So, instead of going home after school and grabbing a microphone to imitate a singer, I grabbed chalk and ink pens to imitate a teacher. I practiced in the mirror, telling children to pay attention to what was on the board, and I would write stories and "lesson plans." I thought being a teacher could lead to influence. Continuing to teach meant continuing to learn, and put truth into power. Teaching would mark my place in the world and would allow me to give and earn respect. My body and spirit changed when I was playing "school" with my older brother, Abdullah—forcing him to be the one and only student in my makeshift classroom.

That energy continued into adulthood, in various roles and positions I took in the field. I was excited while teaching and learning. I created curriculum—although I did not call it curriculum then, that is what it was. I noticed how teaching made me feel. I felt whole and motivated. My mind, energy, and spirit were elevated. No matter what I do in my personal or professional life, I always strive to feel beauty, wholeness, wellness, and happiness.

This is joy.

This is why I do my work in the world for educators—I want them, in their work, to have joy.

As *Cultivating Genius* was growing in popularity, the world was responding to racial and other sociopolitical uprisings across the globe. Citizens protested in the streets against anti-Blackness and other forms of hate. The world was also responding to a global pandemic. Teachers and children moved from the classroom to digital platforms—some were prepared, some had to learn and adjust. I was one of those teachers who had to learn and adjust. Some structures in education had to be paused, such as standardized testing, and some teachers and children felt relief. For some, structures like those are anxiety-producing and don't capture the range of a child's genius.

In those early days of the pandemic, it pained me to lose human contact, but new possibilities opened up, too. Some educators used the freedom to innovate and engage in lessons and units that they may not have tried under traditional pressures, such as the state test. There were educators, too, who addressed the atrocities of the United States, teaching about the lives and deaths of Sister Breonna Taylor and Brother George Floyd. At times, I received emails from teachers telling me they were "in trouble" for teaching lesson plans about Taylor and Floyd, while no leader or parent ever questioned the teaching of other oppressed people, such as Anne Frank. I question the humanity of those who place some injustices front and center, while ignoring others.

With all that was happening in the world, I noticed something: Teachers and children needed joy more than ever, like the ancestors needed joy when their world was in chaos and turmoil. I knew that joy never comes without justice. Educators began leaving the classroom in droves. In *Cultivating Genius,* I explain how the ancestors embraced joy and beauty in their educational pursuits. Joy and beauty were always their goals, as they cultivated their minds, hearts, and loving practices. While writing the book, I even assumed that educators were naturally embracing joy and beauty, and making them their goals.

But in 2020, I felt we all needed to be (more) intentional about (re)claiming joy, in and outside the classroom. So, I returned to the historical archives of Blackness and searched for joy more deliberately. I found multiple accounts of it, dating from before Africans were stolen from the homelands to after they arrived in United States and had to (re)build their lives.

How the Ancestors Embraced Joy

The ancestors embraced joy in many ways—from celebrating life to using their languages and literacies, learning math and science, and creating music and art—before and after striving for freedom (Hannah-Jones, 2021). Joy helped the ancestors to feel whole and, in many ways, provided relief and a purpose for being.

Joy was also solidly connected to their teaching and learning. When I began to read about the centering of joy and justice in historic spaces, such as anti-slavery, benevolent, and literary societies and other collectives, I discovered that many of the ancestors' pursuits carried over to the schools.

The New York African Free School

The pedagogical approaches of the New York African Free School centered joy, as educators sought solutions to society's racism, while centering the truths of students in the elementary and secondary grades. Many members of societies were connected to the New York African Free School, where Black children experienced joy through formal academics. In 1830, Charles C. Andrews, along with the school's administrators, published a book entitled *The History of the New York African Free Schools*, which outlined the schools' philosophies, schedules, and activities. In daily pursuits

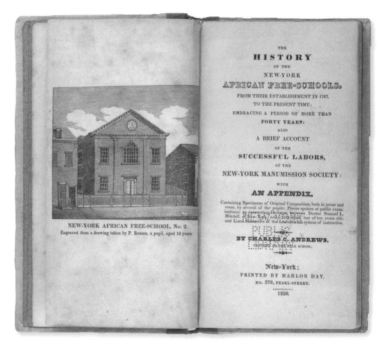

Opening pages of *The History of the New York African Free Schools*

there was a blend of social justice and joy. It was written:

> It is education—it is the cultivation of the mind and the heart which.... leads them [children] to a knowledge of the means, whereby they may insure not only their happiness in the present, but in the world to come (1830, p. 47).

Happiness and joy were important goals of the New York African Free School, yet Andrews and the administrators knew that the way to reach those goals was through abolition, as one educator wrote the same year:

> What is the first requisite in paving the way for the total abolition of slavery? We should answer, *education*. What is the second? And third? —our answer will still be as before—education.

The first African Free School was established in 1787 by white "gradual" abolitionists for free Africans, like several historically Black colleges and universities. The African Free School was followed by organized efforts of the Manumission Society in New York City, whose purpose was to help liberate enslaved people. That one school grew to more schools across the city (Foster, 2004).

The established purpose of the New York African Free School was to resist oppression and racism, and move toward liberation, while imparting to children "the benefits of education, as seemed best calculated to fit them for the enjoyment and right understanding of their future privileges, and relative duties, when they become free men and citizens" (Andrews, 1830, p. 7). Regularly, educators provided notification of student achievement and progress, as well as their promotions in reading, writing, arithmetic, sewing/knitting, elocution, sciences, navigation, astrology, art, and geography. They would have students learn about the state of the world by researching informational texts and writing literary compositions. The publications from which educators designed lessons included:

- *A Father's Legacy to His Children*
- *The Scientific Class Book*
- *Polite Learning*
- *Comstock's and Other Natural History*

- *Scientific Dialogues*
- *Travels at Home*
- *Cook's Travel*
- articles on education, found often in the daily papers

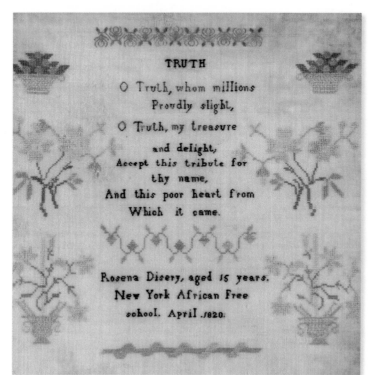

Rosena Disery's poem, "Truth"

The school also lifted and honored children's voices by creating spaces for them to deliver their truths in writing. One common topic for community discussion was called "On Speaking the Truth" (Andrews, 1830). In April 1820, a 15-year-old student, Rosena Disery, wrote and stitched a poem entitled *Truth*, which connects social justice to joy, treasure, and delight.

Children were taught to discuss and write about various topics and issues of the times. Like Black literary societies, all learning was grounded in literacies and language (including reading, writing, thinking, and speaking/communicating). A seven-year-old at the New York African Free School, during this same time, delivered a speech to practice his elocution. Here is a portion of it:

> I am but a little fellow, and know but little. This is my first appearance before you my friends, as a public speaker... I feel a desire to bear my small testimony in favor of the advantages which are derived from a constant attendance at school, and a close application to study while in school, even by the youngest scholar.

The African Free School centered the joy of children by teaching about beauty, aesthetics, and healing, while giving students the space and tools they needed to power their voices. Andrews asked two Black boys to compose poetry on social justice. They wrote:

ON SLAVERY.

Slavery, oh, thou cruel stain,

Thou dost fill my heart with pain:

See my brother, there he stands

Chained by slavery's cruel bands.

Could we not feel a brother's woes,

Relieve the wants he undergoes,

Snatch him from slavery's cruel smart,

And to him freedom's joy impart?

—GEORGE R. ALLEN,
aged 12 years old

ON FREEDOM.

Freedom will break the tyrant's chains,

And shatter all his whole domain;

From slavery she will always free

And all her aim is liberty

—THOMAS S. SIDNEY,
aged 12 years old
(1830, p. 65)

Here, the boys beautifully carried on the tradition of literary Black writers by beginning their titles with the word "On" to emphasize topics that deserved attention and that needed to be captured in time. Their teacher noted that their poems were fully composed and confirmed they were written and signed by the boys (Andrews, 1820). He also noted that young George Allen composed his piece in 30 minutes and Thomas Sidney composed his in one hour. I find both of their writings to be genius and expressions of identity, skills, intellect, criticality, and joy.

The Brownies' Book

The Brownies' Book was a literary magazine developed in 1920 by W. E. B. Du Bois, Augustus Granville Dill, and Jessie Redmon Fauset. It featured stories, plays, letters, poetry, biographies, and other types of texts for children and families (Brooks & McNair, 2008; Harris, 1989). The editors explained in the inaugural issue their purpose:

> It aims to be a thing of Joy and Beauty, dealing in Happiness, Laughter and Emulation, and designed especially for Kiddies from Six to Sixteen. It will seek to teach Universal Love and Brotherhood for all little folk—black and brown and yellow and white.
>
> Of course, pictures, stories, letters from little ones, games and oh—everything!
> —January 1920

Much like literary societies, *The Brownies' Book* had a wide range of ages of youth who benefited from the text. Like Black newspapers, such as the *Freedom's Journal* of the 19th century, it was developed as a platform to center our stories, as well as our joy. During a time when Black children were excluded, stereotyped, and distorted in children's literature, the developers of *The Brownies' Book* desired just the opposite for them. They established the following goals.

- To make colored children realize that being "colored" is a normal, beautiful thing.
- To make them familiar with the history and achievements of the Negro race.
- To make them aware that other colored children have grown into beautiful, useful and famous persons.
- To teach them a delicate code of honor and action in their relations with white children.
- To turn their little hurts and resentments into emulation, ambition, and love of their homes and companions.
- To point out the best amusements and joys and worthwhile things of life.
- To inspire them to prepare for definite occupations and duties with a broad spirit of sacrifice. (Du Bois, 1919, p. 286)

The editors also centered the voices of young people by encouraging them to write for the magazine. Below is a letter by Franklin Lewis, an aspiring architect from Philadelphia.

The magazine filled gaps in texts that were being offered to all children. The collective writings by children were a manifestation of culturally and historically responsive education, back in the 1800s and early 1900s, with joy as a prominent goal. Again and again, for Black communities, a responsive education was the solution to the turmoil of the world. Black educational history continues to be a guide and blueprint for constructively approaching education today. Learning skills was not enough if it had no connection to the world and no direction of making it better.

DEAR MR. EDITOR:

MY mother says you are going to have a magazine about colored boys and girls, and I am very glad. So I am writing to ask you if you will please put in your paper some of the things which colored boys can work at when they grow up. I don't want to be a doctor, or anything like that. I think I'd like to plan houses for men to build. But one day, down on Broad Street, I was watching some men building houses, and I said to a boy there, "When I grow up, I am going to draw a lot of houses like that and have men build them." The boy was a white boy, and he looked at me and laughed and said, "Colored boys don't draw houses."

Why don't they, Mr. Editor?

My mother says you will explain all this to me in your magazine and will tell me where to learn how to draw a house, for that is what I certainly mean to do. I hope I haven't made you tired, so no more from your friend,

FRANKLIN LEWIS, Philadelphia, Pa.

A letter to the editor of *The Brownies' Book* by an ambitious young writer

Black-Centered Schools

Joy continued into the 20th and 21st centuries in communities of color. For example, African- or Black-centered schools carried on the traditions of the New York African Free School. We see this in the history of the Phoenix High School for Colored Youth (1831/1926), Freedom Schools (1964), Clara Mohammed Schools (1980), and countless other schools PreK–12 that specialized in the teaching and learning of diverse identities, skills, intellect, criticality, and joy. Each school carried on traditions of centering and addressing the urgent needs of people of color, giving children the type of education they deserved. Each one was developed from abolitionist pursuits.

Freedom Schools, for example, were initially created by the Student Nonviolent Coordinating Committee (SNCC) in 1964, during the notable Freedom Summer in Mississippi. At the time, most African Americans were offered a sharecropper-based education and few opportunities to gain a broader education. Working with the Southern Christian Leadership Conference (SCLC), founders of the Freedom Schools advocated for and promoted the educational needs of Black children (Muhammad & Moodie, 2022). Much like other schools, the purpose of the Freedom Schools was

to liberate the hearts and minds of students because of the oppression and disproportionality in society that they faced. Each day opened with singing and listening to Freedom Songs to energize them and cultivate their joy. Those Freedom Songs were played, too, during the civil rights movement as anthems to the determination of Black people (Hale, 2011). Like members of Black literary societies, Freedom School students met in churches and other educational spaces to read, write, and think together about racism and an anti-racist society (Hale, 2011).

Joy mattered historically, with and without oppressive conditions. Yet, joy and formal education have never been paired in many spaces. There have been no learning standards for joy, assessments for joy, curricular objectives for joy, teacher evaluations for joy, or a college course on joy in education. Instead, we see remnants of *The New England Primer*, described in Chapter 1. We educators always talk about the importance of joy in teaching and learning, but, still, we rarely see signs of it in our preparation and profession. When teachers and children returned to the classroom as the pandemic numbers declined, they had changed, but curriculum hadn't, for the most part. Many schools simply continued what they were doing before the pandemic. There were few to no classes or college courses on claiming or embracing joy. There were few to no wellness or healing spaces. Too many schools did not offer a robust art program that connected children to the beauty of the earth. That said, when we consider the examples of historical joy I've presented thus far (e.g., New York African Free School, Black Collectives, *The Brownies' Book*, Freedom Schools), we discover lessons we can learn as we go forward.

Now, we must consider how these manifestations of joy show up today and how important they are our for teachers and children.

10 Lessons of Joy From Historical Examples

1. Joy is defined by one's truths, justice, problem-solving, anti-racism, and anti-oppression.

2. Joy is when we define abolition as education and education as abolition.

3. Joy is liberation and liberty for all.

4. Joy is connected to self-determination and self-empowerment.

5. Joy is when we center love, music, and art.

6. Joy is connected to justice and criticality.

7. Joy is present and experienced when learning is collective and collaborative.

8. Joy is enacted when young people's voices and truths are centered and shared.

9. Joy results from cultivating the mind and heart together.

10. Joy is healing from past and present societal harms.

Toward the Pursuit of Joy in Schools Today

In going back to the archives, I added joy as a fifth pursuit to my model of culturally and historically responsive education—the HILL Model—naming all five pursuits because they respond to diverse students' **H**istories, **I**dentities, **L**iteracies, and **L**iberation. In listening to the ancestors (adult and child writers from the 19th century, onward), I found many comprehensive definitions of joy.

Joy is fun and celebratory, yet it is not only about having fun and celebrating in schools and classrooms (although that is important). It is also the embodiment of, learning of, and practice of love of self and humanity, and care for and help for humanity and the earth. Joy encompasses happiness/smiles, truth, beauty, aesthetics, art, wonder, personal fulfillment, and solutions to the social problems of the world.

Joy is also related to advancing happiness by elevating beauty in humanity, as well as embracing truthful narratives and representations of diverse people of the world.

Joy is also related to advancing happiness by elevating beauty in humanity, as well as embracing truthful narratives and representations of diverse people of the world (including our students). When students see themselves manifested in our curriculum in diverse and positive ways, we observe their joy. If students only see a single narrative of who they are—wrapped in slavery, for example—what kind of joy would that elicit? The curriculum should be a mirror (where students can see themselves) and a window (where students can see who they can become—including the achievements associated with people like them) (Bishop, 1990). We also observe their joy when we tell them the truth of the world and give them opportunities to be culturally and historically responsive to those truths.

Joy can and should be an educational pursuit, where we ask ourselves:

- How does my curriculum and instruction enable, amplify, and spread joy (any type of joy)?
- What types of joy could I bring into the curriculum and instruction?
- How does my curriculum and instruction elevate beauty within humanity?
- How will I write learning objectives that will help my students pursue and embrace joy?
- How will I know if my students are experiencing the learning practices of joy?

- How do I begin with—and convey the joy of—Black people and others who have been historically excluded, marginalized, oppressed, misrepresented, or underserved?
- How do I tell the truth and genius about Black people and others who have been historically excluded, oppressed, misrepresented, or underserved?

Joy of people of color is such an urgent pursuit because of efforts to erase it in schools. One cannot fully experience joy if hurt and harm are being inflicted. For example, when I see sisters such as Breonna Taylor shot and killed at home, what safety, beauty, and joy can I fully experience as a Black woman—thinking that such violence could happen to me—unless I am working against such hurt and harm by using my heart (recognizing and feeling the oppression), mind (thinking deeply about the problem), tongue (speaking out against it), and pen (writing out against it)?

Again, joy cannot be embraced fully if oppression is present. Furthermore, if I am personally inflicting hurt and harm on myself with negative self-talk, and someone is attempting to cheer me up and help me to see joy while I simply refuse to interrupt my negative self-talk, can joy enter the moment? This is why a balance of criticality and joy is essential. Joy also balances out the teaching of hard truths and histories, such as Indigenous boarding schools, Asian hate, Islamophobia, the Holocaust, and crimes against women and LGBTQ+ people (to name just a few of so many examples). Groups that experienced those truths and histories had joy before injustices were inflicted upon them. They often used the joy found in painting, music, fashion, and other artistic endeavors to not be overcome with pain. They had happiness, beauty, culture, art, and self-love, even as they were being oppressed. We must begin with their genius, perspectives, and joy, as well as their hard truths and histories.

We should expect joy when we elevate beauty and happiness in the lives of our students when planning and implementing curriculum and instruction. When we center truths about and understandings of the sociopolitical world, students can see themselves fully, and joy can enter their lives.

I consider joy a pursuit—like identity, skills, intellect, and criticality—because it should change and evolve over time, and be student-centered. Unlike "standards," pursuits move students toward the ultimate goals of self-determination, self-empowerment, and self-liberation, and not just success on a standardized test. Standards are stagnant. They are not created by developers steeped in diverse cultures. They are not created for individual learners, whereas pursuits come from and are designed for the learner. Joy is what we (re)member from our childhood and our day-to-day lives as adults. My goal is to help you become more intentional in infusing joy into curriculum and instruction.

Educational Pursuits With Joy as the Ultimate Goal

We need stronger curriculum and instruction that capture the histories, experiences, and priorities of people of color. We deserve curriculum and instruction that is invigorating and rigorous to cultivate the intellectual faculties of children. James Banks (1999) identified four major types of curriculum that vary in terms of their quality and effectiveness: contributions, additive, transformation, and social action.

> 1. **Contributions:** This type of curriculum focuses on surface-level aspects of culture, such as holidays, traditions, food, and heroes and heroines.

It is, therefore, the least effective and most damaging. Identities within humanity are seen as a token (to be put on or removed from a lesson plan). Those who use this type of curriculum see culture as something that lacks intellectual depth. The only time in the year Black culture may be taught, for example, is through Dr. Martin Luther King Jr., and even when that happens, the fullness of his life, joy, scholarship, and abolition is still not taught.

> 2. **Additive:** For this type of curriculum, books and other materials are added to an existing curriculum in an attempt to enhance multicultural content, but curriculum is unchanged. It doesn't include perspectives of children of color.

In several audits across the country, I have found Additive curriculum to be the most popular type of curriculum (not written by teachers), even in cities with rich abolitionist histories, such as New York. Additive curriculum includes (or attempts to include) unit plans that contain some form of multicultural books and ideas, but the objectives, methods, and assessments are not aligned to elements of CRE/CHRE. Merely adding a multicultural book does not equate to CRE/CHRE, nor does it automatically change objectives or assessments. I have seen curricula written only on skills with some suggested and optional multicultural connections. This is especially problematic. Many teachers ask me, *How can I take this curriculum and make it truly culturally responsive?* Before I help, I must first make clear that the content writers never designed the Additive curriculum to be culturally responsive in the first place, and we must ask, *Why have we invested funds, time, and energy in this curriculum? How can we prevent investing funds, time, and energy to a similar curriculum in the future?*

3. **Transformation:** This type of curriculum views issues from multicultural perspectives, and contains more voices. Concepts and objectives include the voices of those who have been distorted or excluded. Students are encouraged to examine and challenge their own views, values, and beliefs.

This type of curriculum is transformative because it involves collaboration and student voice. Students learn from multiple views, histories, and perspectives that we have historically removed or erased from schooling. They center and explore their own beliefs, as they are encouraged to discern between truth and falsehood.

4. **Social Action:** In this type of curriculum, students engage in authentic problem-solving as they explore ways to effect change (Banks, 1999).

The Social Action curriculum builds upon the Transformation curriculum. Together, they are embedded within Gloria Ladson-Billings's framework of CRE as she conceptualized a CRE curriculum as having:

- academics (students learning content, skills, intellect, strategies)
- cultural competence (students learning about their own cultures and diverse cultures of others)
- sociopolitical consciousness (students learning problem-solving through the lens of equity) (Ladson-Billings, 1994; 2014; 2021)

The Social Action curriculum also connects to the practice of using students' genius, cultures, and gifts to create curriculum and teach them more excellently (Gay, 2010). The need for academics, cultural competence, and sociopolitical consciousness stemmed from the historic limitations, low expectations, and mediocrity of curriculum for children of color in schools. The three components of the Social Action curriculum benefit every child, regardless of background. Yet, due to ignorance and hate, there remains a growing effort to ban high rigor. There also remains a wide difference between teachers' backgrounds and students', with 80 percent of teachers being white (Schaeffer, 2021), and a large number of "gradual" abolitionists teaching Black and Brown children.

The Next Generation of CRE Curriculum

A fifth type of curriculum, in addition to Banks's four types, would be a blend of Transformation, Social Action, and joy. I argue for five pursuits for every curriculum to advance strategies and methods. This is the next generation of CRE curriculum that every child needs.

Identity is composed of notions of who we are, who others say we are (in both positive and negative ways), and who we desire to be. There is a complex and dynamic dance between the three toward identity development. Identity isn't static; it is moving and changing. And we don't have just one identity, but layers of them. Identities (cultural and other identities) are constantly being (re)defined and changing. They are fluid, multilayered, and relational, and also shaped by our social and cultural environments, as well as our literacy practices. Our identities encompass many facets, including racial, ethnic, cultural, gender, kinship, academic/intellectual, environmental, personal/individual, sexual, and community.

The focus on identity fosters the learning of individual, family, cultural, and community identities and histories. It also teaches students to know, respect, and value the identities, cultures, and practices of others who may differ from them in any way. Too many schools don't offer students opportunities to learn about the identities of others around the world—others who may be different from them. When teaching children, I avoid saying "different identities" because that language assumes "standard identities." Instead, I try to say, "different from your own identities."

Questions to Consider:
How does my curriculum and instruction (including texts, teacher materials, and learning experiences) help students learn, affirm, and/or validate something about their identity(ies) or the identities of someone else? Which (cultural) identities am I teaching now and why? Which identities have I taught throughout the academic year?

Skills are content-based proficiencies and state standards that empower students to read, write, evaluate, speak, and act confidently, as they seek to imagine and create a more equitable society. Skills are synonymous with competence, ability, and expertise based on what educators deem important to students' learning in ELA and each content area. Skills are what we want students to be able to "do" across content areas, such as cite textual evidence, solve for *x*, question the text, make inferences, and draw conclusions. It's important to remember that state standards are often not rigorous or complete, so they must be adapted and adjusted at times to align with the academic needs of students.

Questions to Consider: *How does my curriculum and instruction (including texts, teacher materials, and learning experiences) help students learn and apply skills independently and meet learning standards for my content area? Which skills and standards am I teaching? Do I need to adapt any state standards to align with students' needs? Are current state standards building on what students already know? What prerequisite skills are needed for these skills to be learned?*

Intellect, or knowledge, is what is learned about various topics, concepts, and paradigms. It is the understanding; exercising and enhancing mental powers and capacities to better understand, as well as critique the world. Therefore, intellect is connected to action. Intellect is connected to the concepts and themes taught in any unit or lesson plan. Intellect also refers to the new interdisciplinary and cultural knowledge students acquire to become "smarter" about something. From W. E. B. Du Bois to Malcolm X to Martin Luther King to Angela Davis, the most influential activists for racial justice have also been intellectuals. Intellect, therefore, is an essential pursuit of the HILL Model designed to inspire young people to be change agents. Students use intellect to connect and apply skills. Intellect is the pursuit that contextualizes the skill to the world.

From W. E. B. Du Bois to Malcolm X to Martin Luther King to Angela Davis, the most influential activists for racial justice have also been intellectuals.

Questions to Consider: *How do my curriculum and instruction (including texts, teacher materials, and learning experiences) help students learn (about) new people, places, things, concepts, and ideas? What kinds of new knowledge am I teaching and why? How does that knowledge connect to the world and help students apply skills in the world? What background knowledge do students already have? What knowledge do they need before I teach new knowledge?*

Criticality asks students to evaluate and dismantle systems of oppression (including, but not limited to, racism, sexism, classism, ageism, xenophobia, ableism, homophobia, and others). Criticality builds social-political consciousness, so students are not passive learners, but rather empathetic, critical thinkers,

working to see, name, and root out discrimination and oppression in all forms. Most important, criticality pushes students to ask how they can liberate themselves, their communities, our nation, and our world from discriminatory and oppressive forces. It requires the ability to read, write, think, and speak in ways to understand power and equity in order to understand and promote anti-oppression, as it relates to the content areas. Unlike "critical" with a lowercase "c," which is just deep, analytical thinking, "Critical" with a capital "c" relates to power, equity, anti-racism, and anti-oppression. As we learn, we must ask, *How am I developing an understanding of power, equity, anti-racism, and anti-oppression?* The ultimate goal of criticality is to help students become sociopolitically conscious beings, and not passive consumers or producers of information. Criticality helps to cultivate a thinker-student. Rather than passively taking in all information as truthful and just, Critical children question and examine multiple positions and perspectives to develop their voice and truths for the betterment of humanity. There are four major categories of criticality that relate to issues of the hurt, hate, harm, and pain afflicted upon:

1. **The environment.** Topics may include pollution, air quality, land acknowledgment, recycling, unjust/inequitable thinking and actions related to taking care of the earth, and other environmental justice topics.

2. **Living organisms.** Topics may include animal abuse, care of plants and other forms of vegetation, and other unjust/inequitable thinking and actions related to living organisms of the earth.

3. **The self.** Topics may include negative self-talk, self-empowerment, self-reflection of negative/imposed views of beauty and mind, and other unjust/inequitable thinking and actions related to self.

4. **Other humans.** Topics may include racism, sexism, religious discrimination, homophobia, classism, age discrimination, ableism, xenophobia, and other unjust/inequitable thinking and actions related to human lives.

A number of criticality topics should be taught throughout the school years, which may depend on student need.

Questions to Consider: *How does my curriculum and instruction (including texts, teacher materials, and learning experiences) help students name, understand, question, and disrupt/interrupt inequities and injustices, such as racism? What Critical topic am I teaching now? Why am I teaching it and why now? What am I disrupting/interrupting? What do my students already know and understand about this topic? What unlearning do they need?*

Joy is the practice of loving self and humanity; caring for and helping humanity and earth; recognizing truth, beauty, aesthetics, art, and wonder; and working to solve social problems of the world. Joy is also about advancing happiness by elevating beauty in humanity, as well as truthful narratives and representations of diverse people of the world (including the narratives and representations of our students).

Questions to Consider: *How does the curriculum (including texts, teaching materials, and learning experiences) elevate beauty and joy? How is joy amplified in each of my unit plans? What forms of beauty, truth, justice, happiness, or benefits appear in what I am teaching? What type or form of joy am I teaching and why? Why do students need this type or form of joy? Why now?*

> *Joy is the practice of loving self and humanity; caring for and helping humanity and earth; recognizing truth, beauty, aesthetics, art, and wonder; and working to solve social problems of the world.*

These five pursuits benefit all children, regardless of their background and skill level. The high-performing child in skills benefits as much as the child who struggles to practice skills independently. The HILL model accelerates the learning of all children by placing their skill development in the context of the global world. If they see purpose of their skill learning, students can connect their learning to humanity and higher-level problem-solving.

Why a Model Derived From Black Excellence for All Children?

I'm often asked if the model is only for Black children. To say these five pursuits are only for Black children would be selfish, and Black people have a history of collaboration, not selfishness. *Have we asked if other scholars' curriculum and practices are only for white children?* When asked why schools should use an educational model for all children derived from Black historical excellence, I focus on these points:

- Historically, Black-centered schools, societies, and other organized spaces were thriving, and have been centers of excellence for learning how to become a stronger and more advanced teacher and leader.
- Black people have brilliantly created, innovated, and found joy amid the harshest oppressions.

- Black diversity and Black history are unique across the world. If we take only Black history in the U.S., the history of chattel enslavement, and the history of building a country, inventing, creating, and developing models, we will learn so much. We use these innovations every day.

- If you want to transform a system for everyone, start with the group for which we have not gotten it right with the most. According to the U.S. data, we fail Black children the most (National Center for Education Statistics, 2021). If we get it right with them, learning from their histories, we gain the experience to advance the state of education for all.

- Black learning goals, or the five pursuits, are more advanced than what we teach today in schools. The five pursuits are greater than just the one.

- The five pursuits teach the whole child, relating to unique identities, qualities, and needs. What child would not benefit from learning about self and others, skills, knowledge, and ways to make a better humanity and create joy?

We have to (re)member, Black is diverse. Often, Black people are seen as monolingual African Americans, but there are African roots in many cultures and languages. For those who do not think culturally and historically responsive education is worthwhile, I don't try to sell it to them. In other words, I don't try to sell the need for humanizing practices, nor do I attempt to get "buy-in" on human lives. If those who don't believe in the five pursuits saw all children's lives as they see their children, we would never debate about the five pursuits. Instead, I ask one question: *What kind of child do you want your school and district to cultivate?* In other words, if you could help a child to "become this" or "develop in this way," what would it be? I've been asking this question of teachers, leaders, and parents for a year, and these have been the most common responses:

- Empathic
- Happy and joyful
- Have knowledge about history and current events
- Have positive mental health and social- emotional intelligence
- Inquisitive
- Kind
- Loves self and others
- Problem-solver
- Skillful across disciplines and contents

- Socially just and conscious when it comes to race, culture, gender, class, ability, and other intersectional identities

The next question I ask teachers, leaders, and parents is also simple: *Will a skills-only curriculum get to the kind of child we seek to develop?* The answer is always no. We cannot say we want the "whole child," but only teach skills, leaving the rest of what that child needs up to chance or to that future teacher who knows how to move beyond skills. We "trick" others by using words such as "balanced," "amplify," and "essentials" to describe curriculum that was not designed to develop the child with these aforementioned qualities.

Students Speak Out

If we listen closely to our students, they will tell us who they are and what they need. We will also find that they deeply desire the five pursuits. As their guest writing educator, I asked middle and high school students from New York City to write two to three sentences explaining who they are, why they write, and the purpose and power of their pens. When they were finished, we put together their statements into a preamble.

We learn here that diverse young people want: 1) more than just test prep and skills; they desire purpose and connection; 2) learning to reflect their lives, while giving them opportunities to learn about and explore the self; 3) to grow, thrive, and experience beauty and joy in learning; 4) social justice, criticality, and an education that helps to build a better world and humanity for all; and 5) no basic education or Additive curriculum, for they are "full of intelligence and creativity" and "levitation." When we compare the children's words to the type of curriculum they typically receive, we see a large gap. In their writing, I also observe the five pursuits:

1. **Identity** (*We are inspirations of beauty; intelligent, creative future leaders; We write to remember ourselves; We are levitation and*

Preamble

We, the Youth Authors, are inspirations of beauty. We use our pens to connect our hearts, share our stories and bring change in the world. Standing here, **we write our hearts out so people can hear the words we might not want to say out loud. Our pens will cross out hate and create spaces for humanity to live in peace—full of intelligence and creativity.** We use our pens to help others be understood. Our pens can connect brains—work as lungs without breath. Our pens can speak, without speaking. Our pens can express what's in our hearts, while mending them at the same time. As future leaders we use **our pens to rewrite a world where we can be one with each other, and harmoniously divine.** It is our joy that fuels it all. **We write to remember ourselves.** For we are **levitation. We represent the next generation.**

represent the next generation.) When children tell us who they are, we must respond by considering how to teach to all the aspects of their lives.

2. **Skills** (*Our pens can connect brains—work as lungs without breath. Our pens can speak, without speaking. Our pens can express what's in our hearts, while mending them at the same time.*) These young authors can combine sentences, vary sentences, use clear and concise language, and build momentum. And they are clearly skilled at using metaphors.

3. **Intellect** (*Full of intelligence. We use our pens to help others be understood. Our pens can connect brains.*)

4. **Criticality** (*Bring change in the world. Our pens will cross out hate. Our pens will rewrite a world where we can be one with each other*)

5. **Joy** (*We write our hearts. Create spaces for humanity to live in peace. Harmoniously divine. It is our joy that fuels it all.*)

These pursuits connect, work together, and build upon each other. My first hope is that students will see themselves in the text, learning while also having space to learn, and accept who they are and resist who they are not (identity). Next, if children know themselves and feel affirmed and safe, my hope is that they will be more prepared and willing to learn skills. Once they have skills, they can apply them in the world (intellect). Once they develop intellect, students can develop a stance—perspectives on how the topic relates to power, control, marginalization, injustice, and inequities. Once they've developed a stance, students are ready to develop criticality at an elevated, more advanced level of thought and learning. After students have learned about a Crit topic and thought about how it affects the state of humanity, they are ready for the beauty, aesthetics, healing, solutions, and other joy-related aspects of learning.

| Identity | Skills | Intellect | Criticality | Joy |

Frequently Asked Questions About the Five Pursuits of the HILL Model

When I visit schools, I am often asked questions about the five pursuits of the HILL Model.

Identity FAQs

1 **Am I supposed to teach about all cultures and identities of all my students?** Implied within this question may be a desire to avoid teaching (about) any culture or identity to children. Hopefully that is never the case. When I hear this question, I get a sense that the teacher is feeling overwhelmed. To answer it, the teacher must first identify how the model is being used. (Chapter 5 offers examples of uses.) The goal is not to teach all the cultures and identities in the world in one single school year, but to connect every lesson, unit plan, or other learning experience to students' lives in some way. By doing that, every learning experience brings children closer to self or to the lives of other people.

2 **What if I don't know (much) about my students' racial, gender, cultural, or other identities?** The simplest answer I offer is, Talk to children and, more important, listen to them. It is important to get to know children in authentic, loving, and meaningful ways so that you learn who they are, who they're not, and who they are destined to become on this earth. If you do not know much about a child's race or other identities, it's important to engage in self-studies and research, honoring who you are as a scholar of the teaching profession. Just as we would not want children to sit in a pool of ignorance, we don't want that for ourselves either. It's important for us to seek knowledge and truths, and read texts (by reliable authors), to understand who our children are.

3 **How do I teach identity in watered-down, scripted curriculum?** Ideally, your curriculum would be rigorous, multicultural, and excellent. However, if it is watered-down and scripted, start by determining the theme or topic of each lesson or unit plan within it. As long as there is a connection to our world, no matter how small, you can then make connections to the identities of your students. Even in simple decodable books or beginner reading books you'll find a person, place, thing, topic, or concept that appears in the context of the world. Once you have it, you can create learning objectives and pursuits where students make connections to their lives.

Skills FAQs

1 **Skills are hard to teach. How do I teach other pursuits along with that one?** Again and again, there is evidence that teaching skills alone is not enough. If the teaching of state standards, proficiencies, and skills is overwhelming, I suggest leaders plan professional learning around content knowledge and methods of teaching. And those leaders may benefit, too, by making it impossible for teachers to fail. Skills may be difficult to teach if they are taught in decontextualized ways and disconnected from students' lives and the world. Are the skills tied only to test prep? In my research, I have found that when skills are taught in concert with other pursuits, such as identity, intellect, criticality, and joy, not only does students' engagement increase, but teachers' professional knowledge and growth do as well. The teaching of other pursuits will never impede the teaching of skills. It will only enhance the teaching of skills—just as teaching and learning in a second language never inhibits the learning of English. It magnifies it.

2 **Who determines which skills "count" or matter in learning?** This has been an interesting question for me, as well as for other teachers. To answer it, I question those who write standards (and tests) adopted by their state or school district. I ask their names, about their backgrounds, and if they are leading educators in the field. I want documented examples of how they have taught diverse children successfully. *What is the relationship between standards writers and test writers?* I encourage you to extend state standards, proficiencies, or skills when they are not rigorous enough.

When skills are taught in concert with other pursuits... not only does students' engagement increase, but teachers' professional knowledge and growth do as well.

Typically, committees determine which skills "count" or matter in learning, and as those committees are developed and organized, we must ask ourselves about the scholarship, theories, models, and frameworks they draw upon to name the skills to be mandated across the content areas to ensure student growth. We must ask whether they go beyond Eurocentric traditions or whether they look wider across communities of color.

3 **How do I find time to teach something other than skills?** Time is a special and interesting construct. We never get it back once it's gone. Time is typically measured in Eurocentric units, and when people don't fall in line with Eurocentric units, they have come up with new labels to measure it, such as "Black or Brown People's Time," which sometimes denotes being "late" or untimely. When we adhere to Eurocentric measures of time, we begin to care less about humanity and more about so-called measures of other people's time.

When genius is centered, time becomes elusive, and creativity and artistic visions push us to rethink moments and spaces. Time is the one thing that teachers need more of, and within my PreK–12 organizational plan for the United States, I would not ask teachers to teach for the entire day, but instead give them more time to cultivate and plan out their genius and joy. We are not going to get more time, but we can use our time differently to teach the five pursuits. And if we teach the pursuits in concert with one another, and not in isolation, we will find that we don't need more time; we will use the time we have more wisely to teach all five pursuits. Several of the pursuits, depending on the learning experience, do not require additional time. Some of them can be practiced as homework, while others can be used to introduce a unit plan in the first few minutes. When we think about time, we must recognize that we can use it differently and creatively to tell the rich curricular stories we are teaching our students.

Intellect FAQs

1 **What's the difference between knowledge and intellect? How do I teach them in mathematics?** Knowledge involves learning new information related to the world. Intellect is knowledge put into action—knowledge that is applied in the world. To connect intellect to mathematics, we must first connect mathematics to the world. One of the purposes of this book is to learn how to become scholars of our content areas or disciplines. Educators must consider issues related to mathematics, including social issues, that can help children learn about new people, places, ideas, and concepts, without sacrificing learning mathematical skills. One helpful approach is to have each mathematics teacher determine one social issue affecting humanity. After determining that issue, ask, *How specifically does math relate to this issue?* From there, create a unit plan about the issue in which students can use math to problem-solve.

2 **What if my state standards in science and social studies feel intellectual enough already?** Science and social studies are two PreK–12 content areas with state standards that contain topics that are written as knowledge-based, while English language arts and mathematics use more actionable language in their standards. When that is the case, we can use intellectual pursuits to extend state standards so that as students are learning science and social studies content, they learn it in relationship to the world around them.

3 **What's the difference between intellect and skills?** We want children to learn skills and actionable proficiencies, and we want them to apply and use those skills independently in the context of the world around them. This is

where intellectualism comes in, where children can take skills and apply them to learning new knowledge, across topics relevant to their lives.

4 **What should I be reading? I feel like I don't know enough in the world to connect skills to intellect.** To cultivate the genius and intellect of our students, we must constantly be cultivating our own genius and intellect. It is impossible to have knowledge of everything, and that is not the goal. The goal is to be constantly seeking and developing our intellectualism. And as we become smarter about various topics of the world, we will more likely be able to discern which sources of knowledge to bring to students. We then become a community of thinkers and a community of learners.

Criticality FAQs

1 **Is criticality only for Black and Brown children?** Every time I hear this question, I think, *What if we thought anti-sexist education was only for girls and women?* Of course, the teaching of criticality, of how to make humanity better, is not just for Black and Brown children. One could argue that other populations that have not been oppressed need criticality the most to build knowledge and empathy. Criticality is for all. It elevates the humanity of all.

2 **Isn't criticality just *critical thinking*?** As mentioned earlier, criticality is more than just critical thinking. It is critical thinking about power, justice, equity, humanity, problem-solving, empowerment, marginalization, and other types of criticality-related topics. Critical thinking is just deep and analytical thinking that may not necessarily involve racism, sexism, homophobia, classism, ageism, ableism, and other types of oppression.

Where we are today should not be where we are tomorrow, if we know that our children need something greater.

3 **What if I am only comfortable teaching certain types of oppression?** Part of the journey toward the HILL Model involves unpacking one's own ideologies and self-reflecting. You may have been socialized to feel comfortable teaching some issues of criticality (such as environmental justice) and not others (such as human justice). At times, I work with teachers who feel comfortable teaching about topics such as "girl power," but not "Black power," or they feel comfortable teaching about the beauty and genius of people who are Black, but not people who are LGBTQ+. Where we are today should not be where we are tomorrow, if we know that our children need something greater. So, part of this work requires extending ourselves and stepping into the *uncomfortable spaces of our minds*. To listen, to learn, and to grow, we must not have a scale of oppression and justice, just

like we must not have a scale of whose injustices, cultures, and lives deserve our attention in the classroom.

Joy FAQs

1 **Isn't joy mainly for children in preschool and elementary school?** To think that joy is reserved only for young children means that, as adults, you may have never desired, needed, or appreciated a sense of joy in ways that I have (re) defined it in this chapter. We need joy like we need water— like we need air to breathe on this earth. Often, joy is not centered in education as children get older, and we know there could be a correlation between that fact and lower levels of achievement as children grow older. Joy is for people at any stage of life, including adulthood.

2 **Is joy just having fun and experiencing happiness in the classroom?** As detailed in this chapter, joy is much more than having fun or experiencing happiness in the moment. It is a sustained sense of fulfillment and happiness. When children experience new adversities or hardship, we want them to be able to bounce back and become resilient beings. Teaching them joy helps with sustained happiness, so they don't fall into sadness or self-defeating spaces. Joy is not temporary. It is sustaining a long-lasting form of happiness, self-liberation, and self-beauty of the mind the heart.

3 **How do I teach joy when I also must teach harsh or painful truths of history, such as the Holocaust, enslavement, Indigenous boarding schools, and the Chinese Exclusion Act of 1882?** You teach to tell the truth. You never start Jewish history (or others who have been oppressed) with what oppressors have done to them. You start the teaching with the histories, genius, and joys of the group of people before oppression, enslavement, or colonization. You tell the truth about their beauty. You must also tell the truth about any human who has harmed another.

4 **How do I teach (about) joy if I don't feel joy?** It is difficult to teach about anything when we do not first recognize it, experience it, or enact it. It may not even be possible. If you are not recognizing, experiencing, or enacting joy in your own life, ask yourself, *How can I bring the beauty of the earth to my students in authentic and holistic ways?* This brings me back to my point about the importance of the self-work that's needed to develop our own identities, skills, intellect, criticality, and joy to create joyful pedagogies in the classroom.

Interrupting for Joy

> "The paradox of education is precisely this—that as one begins
> to become conscious one begins to examine the society in
> which he is being educated."
>
> —JAMES BALDWIN

For humanity to experience joy, we must be conscious of what needs to be interrupted, changed, shifted, and advanced. It is never a question of whether this work is easy or difficult, but instead, Is it possible? And possibility is joy. It is the key to interrupting all that has not served children or educators well. Schools are reflections of society, so as long as there is hurt, pain, and harm in society, we will see them come into our schools, which makes joy even more important. The HILL Model stemmed from research on Black literary societies. *Society* is an interesting word that means "the aggregate of people living together in a more or less ordered community," and we typically think that the wider world, or society, shapes our thinking, language, and actions.

But the ancestors called their abolitionist efforts and organizations "societies," too. They knew the way to genius, justice, and joy was collectivism and collaboration—and organization. They gave us a model and guide for collective, collaborative joy in education. When there is an erasure or historical exclusion of anyone in society, the HILL Model offers a response to it. This model was birthed out of love, history, justice (consciousness), and joy, and when something is created with those four goals in mind, only success and progress can come from it. Students can only benefit when learning is connected to their worlds, identities, and joys. Their test, college, or career prep will not suffer from the teaching of identity, skills, intellect, criticality, and joy. That teaching will only enhance and elevate their lives. In Chapter 3, I focus on how enhancement and elevation begin with the self.

Chapter 2 Reflection

Select one or more questions to engage in a freewrite.

- **What are some reactions and reflections you have about the music, art, and text from Chapter 2?**
- **What ideas and passages stand out for you and why?**
- **What parts do you want to explore further and learn about more?**
- **What parts of the educational system have helped you grow?**
- **What parts of the educational system are in need of water?**
- **What do you plan to do to unearth genius and joy?**

Take some time to color this image.

CHAPTER 3

Unearthing Self

"What we call history is perhaps a way of avoiding responsibility for what has happened, is happening, in time."

—JAMES BALDWIN

LAYERED PLAYLIST

Songs that inspire me about the power of understanding myself and others. Play them as you read this chapter.

"Love's in Need of Love Today," Stevie Wonder

"Greatest Love of All," Whitney Houston

"Man in the Mirror," Michael Jackson

"Beautiful," Christina Aguilera

"Love," Musiq Soulchild

"Ready for Love," India.Arie

"Put Your Records On," Corinne Bailey Rae

"Unwritten," Natasha Bedingfield

"I Know," Jude

"Strength, Courage, and Wisdom," India.Arie

"Freedom is choosing your responsibility.
It's not having no responsibilities; it's choosing
the ones you want."

—TONI MORRISON

Life Is Fine
by Langston Hughes

I went down to the river,
I set down on the bank.
I tried to think but couldn't,
So I jumped in and sank.

I came up once and hollered!
I came up twice and cried!
If that water hadn't a-been so cold
I might've sunk and died.

*But it was
Cold in that water!
It was cold!*

I took the elevator
Sixteen floors above the ground.
I thought about my baby
And thought I would jump down.

I stood there and I hollered!
I stood there and I cried!
If it hadn't a-been so high
I might've jumped and died.

*But it was
High up there!
It was high!*

So since I'm still here livin',
I guess I will live on.
I could've died for love—
But for livin' I was born

Though you may hear me holler,
And you may see me cry—
I'll be dogged, sweet baby,
If you gonna see me die.

*Life is fine!
Fine as wine!
Life is fine!*

Unearthing Thought

1. How's your heart?

2. Who are you? When did you know you wanted to be a teacher and learner?

3. Growing up, what or who shaped your beliefs, values, and thoughts about humanity and those in the world who are often marginalized?

4. What do you know about the genius and joy of Black people and other people of color?

5. When you think about people who have been historically marginalized, what are narratives or labels that need to be unlearned and disrupted?

6. What legacy or imprint do you desire to leave as an educator? How are you working toward it?

7. In what ways are the five pursuits of identity, skills, intellect, criticality, and joy familiar to you? What are your experiences with and beliefs about them?

8. What do you still struggle with when it comes to culturally and historically responsive education?

9. Why do you think there is so much resistance to education rooted in Black histories?

10. When you encounter resistance to culturally and historically responsive education, how do you respond?

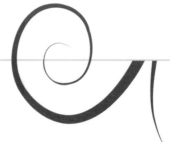

Our Responsibility to Love

Like many readers, I got to know authors Toni Morrison and James Baldwin through their language and the permanence of their written words. Through my reading of their works, and my study of the contexts in which they wrote, I learned the importance of self-identity and self-liberation. They helped me to know myself as I struggled to recognize my genius and worth. They reminded me of who I am and to whom I belong. These authors helped me to love myself and be unapologetic, even in the face of others' hate, ignorance, and failure to recognize my genius. They taught me about responsibility in the world—not just the responsibility we have to know and love ourselves, but also the responsibility to create spaces for the freedom, liberation, and love of others.

Responsibility is an important word, especially when it comes to educating children. Often it is defined as accountability or obligation. Yet, responsibility has also been tied to words such as control and blame. Those inside and outside education pose questions such as, *Who is responsible for student achievement? Who is to "blame" for student failure?* Those questions are not the right ones to ask. It's more important to first turn inward and ask, *Who am I to teach and learn, and to contribute to a better educational system? How do I define responsibility, achievement, and failure in my own life and within the lives of children? What control or influence do I bear in education? Do I feel responsible for what I can't control?*

I chose to start this chapter with the word and concept of responsibility because we are foremost responsible for ourselves, our (un)learning, and our own hearts, before moving toward instructional and practical change. That means that we must engage in self-examination, self-inspection, and self-improvement constantly, which was a historical practice of the ancestors. In the January 16, 1841, issue of *The Colored American* newspaper, writer Uriah Boston published a piece entitled "Self-Examination and Self-Inspection." In it, he states: "Knowledge, in combination with habits of reflection, would lead to self-examination, and self-reflection." Boston speaks to the importance of establishing habits of reflection of ourselves before moving on to the work that we do in the world:

> ...without a habit of reflection and self-examination, we cannot attain a knowledge of ourselves, and without self-knowledge, we cannot apply aright our powers and capacities, correct our failings and defects, or advance to higher degrees of improvement in knowledge and virtue.

Boston goes on to ask several questions of readers, many of whom were in charge of educating children, such as:

> What are the talents and capacities with which I am endowed, and how shall I apply them to the purposes for which they were given me?

Here, Boston encourages us to first reflect on the genius and talents we carry.

> What are the weaknesses and deficiencies to which I am subject, and how are they remedied? What are the vices and follies in which I am inclined, and by what means may they be counteracted?

Here, Boston calls on us to self-reflect on harmful or negative beliefs that we have been subject to or conditioned to believe, and seek ways to overcome them or counteract them with more positive and humane practices.

> How do I stand affected toward my brethren of mankind? Do I hate, or envy, or despise any of them? Do I grudge them prosperity, wish them evil, purposely injure and affront them? Or do I love them as brethren of the same family, and do them all the good in my power, acknowledge their excellencies, and rejoice in their happiness and prosperity?

Boston asks whether we love all of humankind, including those who have been hurt and oppressed most in society. He asks if we love brethren and Blackness as we love ourselves and our own family. I also wondered, Do we want to see certain children fail, or do we instead acknowledge their genius and their "excellencies," and want them to succeed and consequently rejoice in their progress and happiness?

For the Colored American.

SELF-EXAMINATION AND SELF-INSPECTION.

Bro. Ray:—I have read the following extract in Dr. Dick's work on society, and was so edified with it, that I beg leave to present it to your readers, as worthy of their consideration and adaptation. He says, "Knowledge, in combination with habits of reflection, would lead to self-examination, and self reflection. The indolent and untutored mind shuns all exertion of its intellectual faculties, and all serious reflection on what passes within it, or has a relation to moral character and conduct. It is incapable of investigating its own powers, of determining the manner in which they should operate, or ascertaining the secret springs of its actions. Yet, without a habit of reflection and self-examination, we cannot attain a knowledge of ourselves, and without self-knowledge, we cannot apply aright our powers and capacities, correct our failings and defects, or advance to higher degrees of improvement in knowledge and virtue. In order to ascertain our state, our character and our duty, such inquiries as the following must frequently and seriously be the subject of consideration. What rank do I hold in the scale of beings, and what place do I occupy in the empire of God? Am I merely a sensitive creature, or am I also endowed with moral and intellectual powers? In what relation do I stand to my fellow creatures, and what duties do I owe them? What is my ultimate destination? Is it merely to pass a few years in eating and drinking, and in motion and rest like the lower animals, or am I designed for another and a higher state of existence? In what relation do I stand to my Creator, and what homage, submission and obedience ought I to yield to him? What are the talents and capacities with which I am endowed, and how shall I apply them to the purposes for which they were given me?

sarily lead to the most beneficial moral results. Brethren, read them, and profit by them, and always have them in your minds.

Uriah Boston.

Uriah Boston's piece in the January 16, 1841, issue of *The Colored American* newspaper

Self-Examination and Self-Inspection

The work of self-examination and self-inspection, as well as the questions posed by Uriah Boston, are all part of the responsibilities with which we have to teach, lead, and learn alongside our students. The concept of responsibility is key to the CHRE Model because the model itself is a response to the needs of the children and the social times, but it is also a *responsibility* to the earth. James Baldwin reminds us that the current state of the world (which includes schools) connects to the past, and failing to recognize the accurate history that has led us to where we are today could desensitize us to the issues and needs of young people. He rhetorically asks, *Is it actually "history" if it is still happening in real time?* We must name, understand, question, and disrupt "real-time" histories that are currently happening and problematic. Likewise, Toni Morrison reminds us that freedom is connected to responsibility. She also pushes us to consider the responsibilities we have as humans and as educators helping to cultivate future generations of children.

The work of responsiveness and responsibility must begin with love—a love of ourselves and one another. I have found love to be the answer to any educational dilemma, and often wonder about those who write mandates and policies. What role does love play in their work? Do they consider and discuss love when they're writing? The pandemic taught me so much about love of humanity. When the world shut down and people began experiencing severe hurt and loss, I shifted my meeting agendas. Instead of getting to the day-to-day, work-related items, I asked teachers questions such as, *How's your heart? What is the light in your life?* and *How are you (re)claiming your joy today?* I began to tell teachers and leaders that I love them more often. When they hurt, I hurt. When they were triumphant, so was I.

Do we want to see certain children fail, or do we instead acknowledge their genius and their "excellencies," and want them to succeed and consequently rejoice in their progress and happiness?

Love isn't a competitive act. It isn't about who has the best lesson plan or the highest evaluation. It is, instead, collective and in the spirit of the South African concept of "ubuntu," which means, "I am because we are." Love is interrupting the numbness and distance we feel when others are oppressed, hurt, or harmed. So many teachers struggle with culturally and historically responsive instruction because of a lack of love for themselves and for their children—not only their students, but all children across humanity. I remember reading the newspaper report about when our young child, Trayvon Martin, was shot and killed. The writer questioned his clothing choice that morning. The writer did not question why a grown man hunted down and killed a young child. Those who struggle with culturally and historically responsive instruction, I am reminded, may not see Trayvon Martin as their own. Yet, Trayvon Martin was mine. I never met him, but he was my son, my nephew, my student. I saw him as part of my own humanity. I loved him. Others who struggle with this work may never love him. And if you cannot love an innocent child, it may be difficult or impossible to love yourself. This work starts with love—loving yourself, being yourself, being kind and gentle with yourself, and showing yourself grace as you carry out this work. This will hopefully lead to having the capacity to love other people's children.

This work also begins with loving our children no matter how they come into this world and no matter how they grow into this world. Even if their ideologies or cultures do not align with our own ideologies or cultures, we must still love them. Even if they don't love the disciplines we teach, we must still love them. If we do not love ourselves or love all our children, we will find no method, theory, or strategy to overcome pedagogical struggles. Therefore, we must turn to responsibility and reflect on ourselves, our students, and our thinking and actions. Yolanda Sealey-Ruiz (2022) calls this process an archaeological unpacking and "digging" of self, each human accepting the call to engage in self-examination and self-reflection to improve before teaching and learning with children.

Our Responsibility to Reflect and Unlearn

I often wonder if we humans can pinpoint the exact moment in our lives when we felt comfort and true knowledge of self—when we felt safe and at peace, a sense of belonging to the earth. When we feel such self-freedom, we give up meaningless things that others may value—things that do not advance humanity. We care less about trivial things, capitalism, state exams, and physical objects, and care more about hearts and human-thriving. To get to that place, we must know about the world, the world's beautiful diversity of humanity, who we are in the context of the world, and what the earth needs. We must have the skills to navigate the world and claim our own joy.

There actually may not be one single moment to pinpoint, but multiple moments in our lives when we come to self. Coming to self means knowing our identities and becoming unapologetic about who we are—having humble entitlement about our beauty, genius, and justice orientations. Coming to self means not just knowing ourselves today, but also knowing who we are destined to be—knowing our purpose on the earth. It means being conscious of the world around us and knowing what drives our thinking, decision-making, and actions. It means not just understanding our own struggles and adversity, but recognizing the struggles and adversity of others, and empathizing.

As educators, we have a great responsibility to cultivate knowledge, reflect upon our lives, and be able to name our purpose for and approach to teaching and learning. When I was in high school, I was given no literature or classroom learning objectives designed to help me come to self—to celebrate my Black girlhood and discover the genius of my history and of my future. I was never asked, *Who are you?* or *How is this learning shaping your personal development and life?* When I was preparing to become a teacher, my preservice program offered not one single course where I could reflect and unpack myself, my racial and cultural identities, and my journey through the construction of my ideologies. As a result, I struggled to explain my instructional practices. Such a course could have helped me to name, understand, reflect upon, and conceptualize my:

- upbringing
- PreK–12 education
- values, beliefs, and ideologies, and the context in which I constructed them
- thinking that didn't help to advance humanity
- thinking that served humanity well
- liberatory wellness
- thinking, decisions, and actions that have been normalized
- thoughts about people who have been marginalized on the earth (such as Black people, Indigenous people, people of color, women, members of the LGBTQ+ community, and others) and how I had come to learn about humanity
- conception of media and how it influenced my thinking about myself and others

These are examples of reflections of self that shape how we approach education. One college course on the self is certainly not enough to arrive at deep, personal understandings. Yet, for me, it would have been a useful starting place to figure out what grounds my approaches with children—how I would one day communicate and teach them.

Disrupting What Has Been Normalized

Often, we teach in the same ways we were taught, whether we are teaching reading, writing, math, science, or history. We have been socialized to avoid disrupting what has been normalized. Perhaps that is why curricula and evaluations without language related to anti-racism and equity continue to survive. We have also been socialized not to reflect on, think or talk about, or disrupt topics related to race, gender, sexuality, culture, and oppression, and have instead been socialized to maintain norms of what many have called "Eurocentric or dominant cultural ways of life." In *Why Are All the Black Kids Sitting Together in the Cafeteria?*, Beverly Daniel Tatum (2003) points out that we have been socialized to avoid talking about race. As a result, our children have come to value whiteness and white ways of being and living in the world. Whiteness has grounded the types of curricula we select (or don't), the teaching approaches and theories we embrace (or don't), and what we consider valuable enough to teach, measure, and assess. The fact that we mostly (if not only) teach, measure, and assess skills proves that we have not done a great job of disrupting the system so that it recognizes the values of people of color, specifically Black children whom we have struggled the most to educate in the United States. When a racialized event happens to us as children, it's often traumatic because the adults in our lives have not cultivated race-consciousness and taught us about the beauty and genius of humans of different races from our own. Tatum adds:

> ...the Black child absorbs many of the beliefs and values of the dominant White culture, including the idea that it is better to be White. The stereotypes, omissions, and distortions that reinforce notions of White superiority are breathed in by Black children as well as White. Simply as a function of being socialized in a Eurocentric culture, some Black children may begin to value the role models, lifestyles, and images of beauty represented by the dominant group more highly than those of their own cultural group (p. 76).

We have been socialized to use certain language and embrace certain beliefs, too. So, as we engage in self-work, we must be willing to *unlearn*. It is essential for us to unlearn deficit thinking—thinking that imposes great limitations upon various groups within humanity. I often remind teachers with whom I work, as well as myself, that we are interrupting the same system that many of us were educated and socialized within. That calls for an unlearning of practices, theories, and methods that have not served all students well. We also must help children to unlearn any type of self-hate, stereotyping, and limitations that they have been socialized to believe.

Unlearning Deficit, Limited, or False Narratives of People of Color

When people who have been marginalized in society—including people of color—are erased, deficit, limited, or false narratives of them are taught in schools. Those narratives must be unlearned and replaced with respectful, honest, and truthful language about children. Consider these moves.

Instead of Saying...	Say...
at-risk	genius
unmotivated child	a child in an unmotivating curriculum
struggling students	struggling instruction, assessments, policies, and systems of education
the child is strange or weird	the child is genius and creative
defiant and confrontational	genius
non-English speaker	"child's language(s)" speaker e.g., Spanish speaker, Pashto speaker
non-white	naming who they are
subgroup	naming who they are
minorities	naming who they are
red student/RTI Tier 3	genius
grit	genius
underdeveloped skills	full genius developing
low-functioning child	low-quality assessments
family instability	societal instability
remediation	systematic problems
poor attitude toward school	unclear purpose of school and the extent to which it is fulfilling our students' lives and joy
celebrating resilient students	creating spaces where students don't have to overcome the curriculum and instruction they've been handed
not a math person	every child a math person
disadvantaged child	disadvantaged systems and structures
can't read/nonreader	student who is struggling at the moment with a particular skill or strategy (e.g., letter-sound relationships)
traditional "achievement data"	wider equitable achievement data
labeling ancestors as slaves	referring to them as geniuses who were forcibly enslaved
Why did the parents give their child that name?	What a beautiful and original name!
test prep	cultivation of students' genius and joy

What other shifts in language have you made or do you need to consider making?
Some of these terms are so highly coded within a school or district that, on the surface, they may not feel inequitable or deficit. So, we must ask, is the term capturing a complete and accurate depiction of children? The language we use, our beliefs in humanity, and our ideologies matter because they impact our practices, and children know when they are not respected or loved, or if their genius is not centered. Consider other terms related to our children that could use unlearning.

Unlearning Deficit or Basic Instructional Practices

Each content area has a tradition of how it has been taught and promoted in schools. We must study traditions and decide whether they are excellent, basic, or deficit. We may be inflicting harm without knowing it—such as when we teach only skills. When we consider traditional pedagogies in reading and math, an unlearning of those pedagogies is needed. Both disciplines have a history of focusing solely on the "cognitive sciences" or skills-only teaching and learning.

TRADITIONS IN READING AND LITERACY AND MATHEMATICS

We still define reading and literacy as skills or as something students have or don't have. But the ancestors have taught us that reading and literacy are more expansive and are directly connected to the five pursuits: identity, intellect, criticality, and joy, as well as skills. They are connected, too, to self, the world, liberation, and freedom, yet most approaches to reading development, especially early reading development, are decontextualized and absent of identity and criticality (and at times, intellect and joy, too).

Researchers have argued for broader literacies across PreK–12 that connect more to sociopolitical consciousness and the sociocultural environment. "Reading instruction," Gee (2001) writes, "must be rooted in the connections of texts to engagement in and simulations of actions, activities, and interactions—to real and imagined material and social worlds" (p. 716).

Much like reading pedagogies, mathematics has traditionally been decontextualized from the lives of students, racial justice, and the humanities. While there has been an effort (Lerman, 2000) to make math education more inclusive of sociocultural learning, we still see frequent examples of it being taught from a skills-only standpoint, disconnected from applications in the sociopolitical world. That effort has certainly brought more social justice and criticality into math learning, and adding identity, intellect, and joy can also extend the discipline further.

When we unlearn the traditions that have created limitations, we may begin to extend the skills to be contextualized to students' identities, intellect, criticality, and joy. For example, we can extend a traditional lesson plan about decoding while still teaching, modeling, practicing decoding skills (within the science of reading). Several reading programs are written for children to develop literacy in ways that are disconnected from multicultural literature, their lives, interesting themes, and social justice. Perhaps creators of those programs think we can't cultivate reading sciences or skills along with identity, intellect, criticality, and joy into one program. Take how we typically teach students to decode unfamiliar words. We ask them to a) study the parts of the word, b) isolate the consonants and vowels, c) chunk the word into syllables and say them, d) listen for the word, and e) clap and say the whole word. We may then prompt students to practice with more words in isolation.

One way to adapt or extend this approach for grades 2–3 as an example, is to select a theme to teach, such as "vacations," or "summer," and select quality multimodal texts with decodable words such as *vacation*, *experience*, *expedition*, *excursion*, *photographs*, *reservations*, and *transportation*. Then you may teach the pursuits along these lines:

> **Identity:** Students will identify what they would like to do or where they would like to go on a vacation.
>
> **Skills:** Students will learn how to decode multisyllabic words.
>
> **Intellect:** Students will learn about different types of vacations.
>
> **Criticality:** Students will learn about the importance of access and opportunity related to vacationing.
>
> **Joy:** Students will identify their favorite vacation-related word and decode it.

For extended learning, you may engage students in read-alouds, using books such as:

- *Imagination Vacation* by Jami Gigot
- *One Hot Summer Day* by Nina Crews
- *Tar Beach* by Faith Ringgold
- *A Lullaby of Summer Things* by Natalie Ziarnik
- *Blackout* by John Rocco
- *Jabari Jumps* by Gaia Cornwall

This approach *unlearns* the notion that we can't teach according to the science of reading if we include culturally and historically responsive pedagogies. We can, in fact, teach early reading skills while also teaching other pursuits of identity, intellect, criticality, and joy.

Redefining and Expanding Notions of Genius and Joy

The work of CHRE has led us to redefine and expand notions of genius and joy. I have had to unlearn certain definitions of those two words as I began to research and write *Cultivating Genius* and this book.

GENIUS

If we think about the word *genius*, most of us may picture older white men, such as Albert Einstein. We have been socialized that genius refers to a few selected among us who have scored high on a measure that was not developed with Black or Brown genius in mind. And when Black and Brown genius is erased, folks make the assumptions that it doesn't exist, or has never existed. Genius has been seen as rare, and that perception has isolated children who have their own special gifts and talents. Although that outdated definition of genius became the norm in modern society, our ancestors had different meanings—they redefined genius.

JOY

Joy is not a fleeting feeling of happiness, but a sustained sense of fulfillment and self-determination, self-liberation, and self-empowerment. While happiness may be temporary, joy is long-lasting, and having it helps us to be calmer and more resilient when adversity or disappointment comes into our lives. This work we do in education is not just about graduating students or ensuring they pass state assessments; it is about human development and helping children *come to self* and recognize and celebrate their own genius. Before we can do that well, though, we must reflect on ourselves as educators. Ask yourself:

- What are examples of thinking and practices that I need to discard, transform, or extend?
- What schematic knowledge do I need to have that works?
- What do I need to unlearn about people of color and other people who have been historically neglected?
- What do I need to (re)member, and/or return to when it comes to genius beliefs and practices?
- What do I need to disrupt?

- As I am unlearning, how do I normalize new ways of thinking, acting, and teaching?
- What racist, sexist, discriminatory beliefs have been conditioned inside of me from family, community, and society (literature, media, etc.)?
- Can I say "Black Lives Matter" out loud, in public? Why or why not?
- What would my colleagues say about me?
- What thoughts and ideals do I need to disrupt?
- Do I only care for the people who share my beliefs?
- Who are the people I keep close to me?

Reflection Pathways to Unearth Knowledge of Self and Students

In this section, I provide reflection pathways for unearthing and coming closer to yourself and your students. You can answer the questions on your own, in small (and safe) discussion groups, or through critical writing.

Yourself

My Identities

1. Who am I?
2. What racial, cultural, and other identities do I identify with?
3. What have I come to understand about my different identities?
4. Have I ever experienced marginalization related to my identities?
5. Am I an anti-racist educator? Do others recognize racial justice in me, or do I only see it in myself?
6. What is the related genius and joy connected to my identities?
7. When did I discover who I am, and how did that feel? When did I come to self?
8. Why does identity matter in PreK–12 education?
9. Whose identities have been taught and not taught in schools?
10. When it comes to racial and cultural identities, what have I learned about diverse people?
11. What have I learned about Black and Brown excellence and genius?
12. Is identity development possible in PreK–12 schools? How might I connect the teaching of identity to art, health, math, science, English language arts, social studies, or other content areas?

continued

My Identities *continued*

13. What is one significant memory I have of a teacher (growing up) connecting pedagogy to one or more of my identities? How did that feel?
14. How does identity show up in my pedagogy and leadership?
15. How do I plan to learn more about my identities and the identities of others?

Start with one question and write down your thoughts.

My Skills

1. Why did I choose to teach this content area?
2. What is my self-efficacy in this content area?
3. What have I read and written related to my discipline?
4. Which scholars or thought leaders reflect my beliefs, methods, and practices?
5. Why do skills matter in PreK–12 education?
6. Why do I think the system is only designed to teach and measure skills?
7. Why aren't skills enough for human development?
8. Which skills do I/did I use from PreK–12 education? Which didn't I use?
9. How do skills show up in my pedagogy and leadership?
10. Do I believe that the teaching of skills alone is too difficult to add other pursuits?
11. How can I begin to contextualize the skills I teach to relate to students' lives and the world we live in?
12. What are some helpful methods, strategies, or approaches for teaching skills?
13. How do my students learn skills best? What helps them when learning new skills?
14. How can I relate state standards to any topic or theme in the world?
15. How do I plan to learn more about pedagogical skills of teaching and learning?

Start with one question and write down your thoughts.

My Intellect

1. What does intellect mean to me?
2. Am I a scholar of my discipline?
3. Why is intellect essential in PreK–12 education?
4. How do I develop my own intellectualism related to my content area?
5. What interesting knowledge do I already carry?
6. Who has cultivated my genius and knowledge about the world?
7. What topics have I always wanted to teach (about)?
8. What do I know about the (cultural) history of the discipline(s) I teach?
9. How do I see the world in art, music, health, math, science, language, or history?
10. Which topics, themes, people, places, concepts, etc., did I learn as an adult that made me ask, *Why didn't I learn this in K–12 education?*
11. Do I understand the difference between skills and intellect?
12. What historical and contemporary topics are worthwhile for teaching?
13. What topics would my students like to learn about?
14. How does intellectualism show up in my pedagogy and leadership?
15. How do I plan to learn more about new topics of the world for teaching?

Start with one question and write down your thoughts.

My Criticality

1. What do I know about criticality and critical theories?
2. Where are my consciousness and anti-oppression thinking/practices?
3. What injustices have I seen or experienced in the world?
4. Which injustices haven't I seen or experienced in the world?
5. Do I believe I have to experience an injustice to know it is real and important to humanity?
6. Are there topics related to criticality that I am comfortable or uncomfortable teaching?
7. Is there a place for justice, power, anti-oppression, and equity topics in schools? Where?
8. Why should we teach students to have sociopolitical consciousness?

continued

My Criticality *continued*

9. What are five social problems or issues that connect to the discipline I teach?
10. What long-term benefits are offered with criticality teaching?
11. Why do I think some people are against criticality teaching?
12. What if others don't invite or support my teaching of criticality?
13. What is one significant memory I have of a teacher connecting pedagogy to justice or social change?
14. How does criticality show up in my pedagogy and leadership?
15. How do I plan to nurture my criticality?

Start with one question and write down your thoughts.

My Joy

1. What does joy mean to me?
2. What gives me joy?
3. What gives me joy for this profession?
4. How do I cultivate my own joy as a professional?
5. Who cultivates my joy?
6. Growing up, what gave me joy in schools—that helped me to learn?
7. Do I understand the forms of beauty that relate to my discipline?
8. Why is joy essential in PreK–12 education?
9. Why is joy perceived as an unserious/unimportant learning goal sometimes?
10. Is joy only for early childhood and elementary education?
11. Where is my own joy today?
12. How do my students experience joy in the classroom?
13. What are some helpful methods, strategies, or approaches for teaching joy?
14. How does joy show up in my pedagogy and leadership?
15. How do I plan to engage in and sustain my joy?

Start with one question and write down your thoughts.

Your Students

My Students' Identities

1. Who are my students?
2. How have I or will I plan to get to know them?
3. What racial and cultural identities do they identify with?
4. Have they ever experienced marginalization related to their identities?
5. What is the related genius and joy connected to their identities?
6. What do I know about their ancestral genius, justice/abolition, and joy?
7. Do they want school to be a place to learn about self and others?
8. Do they feel loved and seen in our classroom?
9. Do they struggle or excel with a strong sense of self?
10. What areas of self would they like to cultivate?

Start with one question and write down your thoughts.

My Students' Skills

1. Are my students in love with the content area we teach and learn?
2. What is their self-efficacy in this content area?
3. What have they read and written related to the content area?
4. How do they learn skills best?
5. When learning something new, what helps them to excel?

Start with one question and write down your thoughts.

My Students' Intellect

1. What do my students already know?
2. What is their genius?
3. What do students want to learn about (topics) in school?
4. Where do students cultivate their knowledge of the world outside of school?
5. Do students want to learn how to apply skills to the real world?

Start with one question and write down your thoughts.

My Students' Criticality

1. Where are my students' consciousness and thinking about oppression?
2. What injustices have they seen or experienced in the world? What injustices have they not seen or experienced in the world?
3. Do they want school to be a place to learn about justice and what it takes to build a better world for all?
4. Are students able to distinguish between truth and falsehood in the world?
5. What social change would students like to see within humanity?

Start with one question and write down your thoughts.

My Students' Joy

1. Do my students have joy in the classroom learning?
2. How do I know when my students experience joy?
3. Do they understand the forms of beauty in the world?
4. Do they want to learn about beauty, truth, and happiness?
5. What artistic and creative sensibilities do my students have?

Start with one question and write down your thoughts.

Answering these questions will help you build positive and respectful relationships with your students. In time, they will see their classroom as mini-literary societies and intellectual feasts, where they can connect their learning to the world and needs of humanity.

Our Responsibility to Respond to CHRE Resistance

When working with educators across the world, I am often asked:

- How do you respond to people who do not want to engage in equity or justice-centered work?
- How do you convince them to get on board with or to buy into this work?

There are a few things we must first understand before responding to these questions. First, I interrupt the "on board" and "buy into" language because it objectifies humanity. We are talking about human lives and, therefore, must choose our words with great care. I should not have to sell this work or ask for "buy-in." We are not buying tangible things. We are referring to human lives and humanizing practices. Similarly, I should not have to convince educators that academic success, identity, justice, and joy are good for children. Those educators should already know that from being well-read in education. It is like my mother convincing me that water is good for me. She should never have to do that. *I should just know, right?* I should know that, in order to live, one must drink a healthy amount of water. Yet, we still must "convince" others that CHRE is good for teachers, leaders, and students.

As a young child, I learned about a Hadith, or a story, in Islamic culture that taught me how to respond to any form of harm, hurt, or pain on earth—including in educational practices. The Hadith taught me that one way of responding is to empathize with those who have been harmed. Another way is to use my words, spoken or written. Although it is not always easy, I strive to speak up and out against injustice and for justice and joy. This book is yet another example of me applying lessons learned from the Hadith. Using my words is my purpose and responsibility, and I believe educators must consider if it is theirs, too. As a teacher educator, I am responsible for teaching adults. Yet you may feel as a PreK–12 teacher you weren't hired to teach other adults. Yet you still must be prepared to respond when adults resist or don't understand this work. This work is difficult if one doesn't have the humanity for it or hasn't done the critical self-work that I described earlier in this chapter.

So, in this section, I walk you through a process of responding. I provide questions I ask myself and others to understand perspectives. I try to make sure my responses to those who do not support the work are appropriate, loving, respectful, honest, and bold.

1 **What are you against?** The first thing I seek to understand from those who are against this work is: *What exactly are they against?* The HILL Model gives us the language to walk through the purpose of each pursuit and ask clarifying questions:

- Are you against children learning about themselves and the cultural lives of others? (Identity)
- Are you against children learning the state standards and proficiencies across different content areas? (Skills)
- Are you against children learning new knowledge related to the global world? (Intellect)
- Are you against children learning how to name, understand, and disrupt injustices? Are you in favor of some injustices being taught and others not? Why? (Criticality)
- Are you against children learning about and experiencing beauty and happiness in schools and classrooms? (Joy)

These questions help me—and will help you—get to the root of what people do not support. Often, people rely on sensational reporting in the media to form opinions and make decisions about education. But it's important for us to take moments to read and study deeply what those people are for and what they are against.

2 **What have you read recently that relates to what you are for and what you are against?** This leads me to my next questions: *What have you read to center your understanding of justice, equity, and culturally responsive pedagogy? When was the last time you wrote a CHRE lesson or unit plan and taught it? If educators have not read the work of pioneers of CRE, how do they know what they are against? And can they be against something they have no or limited knowledge of?* There is much falsehood in the media related to culturally responsive work, justice-oriented learning, and critical race theory, and those who are taking in that information often do not turn to primary source documents and scholarship related to the work. Some have never even written or taught a CHRE lesson or unit plan. If we are to engage in healthy debate, we must be prepared for the debate. I ask: Do those who oppose CRE know enough to debate those who have engaged in reading and scholarship? Educators must be well-

If we are to engage in healthy debate, we must be prepared for the debate.

read—especially those who serve in leadership roles. If you lead, you must read! I often ask: *How can one resist something so beautiful—something that will only enable the earth (and those who inhabit it) to grow?* Yet, some still don't understand institutionalized and systematic racism, and how it has grown and spread. Without that understanding, it may be difficult to grasp other topics of criticality.

3 **Why do you resist the five pursuits?** Next, I try to get at the root of why some people may not support the five pursuits. Typically, they resist the work for four major reasons.

- **Lack of knowledge or ignorance about what this work entails.** As I said, this work requires us to cultivate our intellect and genius by reading and studying scholarship related to it. So many people equate CRE/CHRE with being anti-white people or anti-white children, and nothing could be further from the truth. They think CRE/CHRE is only for Black and Brown children. Yet, we know that schools have been greatly underserving white children as well by not teaching them about criticality and the genius of Black and Brown people.

- **Fear of failure.** Some teachers fear their practice will suffer if they begin to teach in these ways, or that their students will not gain the required skills needed to pass the state exam. While we know the state exam provides access to many opportunities such as college and careers, we also know that the HILL Model does not disrupt their preparation for such opportunities. Teachers may also fear that they don't know enough, and they may be evaluated as "struggling" or "inadequate." But this should not be about what we fear, but rather what children deeply need and desire, and cultivating our professional knowledge to deliver excellent instruction.

- **Teacher burnout.** Teachers are frequently stressed and overwhelmed, and some don't welcome additional learning or work for children. Sometimes, they recognize the beauty and the strength in the five pursuits, yet they continue comfortably with mediocre or basic learning practices. Again, this work is not so much about the comfort of the teacher as it is about the needs of students.

- **Hate for any model related to Blackness.** During the pandemic, I gave a workshop to parents in a northeastern urban city. As part of it, I talked about justice and joy, and how to create experiences at home that support the five pursuits, with an emphasis on joy. I shared 20 "joy activities" for the home, using "making slime" as one of the examples. I explained the science and joy behind slime-making. And I told them about the beautiful colors and textures that can be created with children. I have my daughter to thank for teaching me this. In that moment, one of the parents wrote privately in the chat: "This is awful—you are awful." I wondered if there was some sort of oppressive history involving slime. No. This parent hated the fact that I showed up as a Black woman, in my full genius and joy, knowing who I am and whose I am. I wondered why the parent did not choose to share her comment publicly. If we hurt and hate someone so boldly, why not share those feelings with the superintendent, principals, and other parents who were there? Often, I find that just showing up mentioning genius and joy as a Black woman is enough to trigger acts of hate and resistance. The woman likely would not have said "you are awful" to a white woman talking about slime. This parent did not care if my feelings were hurt or that she harmed another human. I wonder what happens when parents like these show up for their own children. *What are those parents not teaching their children? Has this parent ever taught her child to know and love Black women? Who will her children become as adults, and how will that adult contribute to humanity?* This was not the first time I have experienced or witnessed hate. This is why this work is so complex. It doesn't just involve cultivating the mind, but the love in one's heart as well.

When school leaders tell me they have high-achieving students and methods that are already working, I often ask: Working for whom?

The first three reasons for resistance open opportunities for critical learning and unlearning if one's mind and heart are open. As a leader—for teachers who are stressed and overwhelmed, and do not want to try a new approach—I co-construct a lesson or unit plan with them and co-teach it. I make it easy and try to make it impossible for them to fail, and together we collect data and responses from students related to their engagement and achievement.

4 **Is what is currently happening in your school "working"?** When school leaders tell me they have high-achieving students and methods that are already working, I often ask: *Working for whom?* I find that students who come into schools as academic achievers will sustain their success. But are all children achieving and not just in skills and intellect, but in identity development, criticality, and joy as well? If so, I would encourage those leaders to continue their pathway, if we have evidence of that success across diverse youth. The HILL Model was never designed to replace anything that is working well and serving all children to the highest level of excellence.

5 **What do you desire most for the development and advancement of children?** Often, teachers, parents, community members, and leaders want children to grow personally and academically. They want children to be loving,

happy, empathetic, critically thoughtful, and skillful, and to be great contributors to and citizens of the world. Yet, they oppose the model that actually prepares children to be all those things.

Below is a short list of questions I ask stakeholders—five simple questions. If they answer no to any of them, we have conversations, and often they have to go back to doing the self-work for our hearts and for self-love.

- Would you like schools to help your child have strong knowledge of self and others? (Identity)
- Would you like schools to help your child learn content area skills and state standards? (Skills)
- Would you like schools to help your child gain knowledge about the world? (Intellect)
- Would you like schools to help your child learn how to problem-solve and make the world a better place? (Criticality)
- Would you like schools to help your child learn about and experience beauty and happiness in the world? (Joy)

The truth of the matter is, these five pursuits have only made this earth better. There is a great deal of kindness, equity, creativity, inquiry-based learning, problem-solving, and social-emotional learning that connects to the model. When people resist this work around anti-racism and justice, it's difficult not to take it personally because of the nature of it and its connection to my own racial identity and histories; yet, I seek to get to the root of the resistance and try to educate.

Our Responsibility to Our Children

> "We all have a certain measure of responsibility to those who have made it possible for us to take advantage of today's opportunities."
>
> —ANGELA DAVIS

We cannot teach who we don't know. Nor can we teach students to know themselves, their consciousness, or their joy if we don't know ourselves, our consciousness, or our joy. By beginning the work with the self, we move toward liberatory wellness and joy, which we educators need and deserve. Liberatory healing self-work begins with knowing our identities and to whom we "belong." That self-work helps us (re)member who we are and why we do the work we do in the world. I encourage you to make a list of people who have positively influenced you (past and present), read their works and read their lives, and spotlight quotes and sayings that define your profession and your identity as pedagogues and leaders. I close with my own list with hopes that it inspires and reminds you of who you are, and our shared responsibility to the children.

Who Are You and Who Do You Belong To?

I AM a conductor, and I belong to Sister Harriet.

> "I was the conductor of Underground Railroad for eight years, and I can say what most conductors can't say—I never ran my train off the track and I never lost a passenger."
>
> —HARRIET TUBMAN

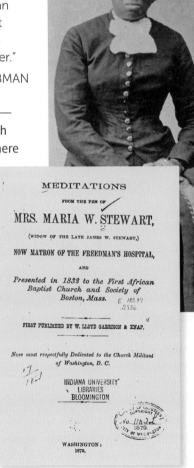

When your heart is stressed, don't give up— keep going back and cultivating the growth of our students, helping them to get to where they need to be, and honoring their full potential.

I AM a leader, teacher, and a doer of my word, and I belong to Sister Maria.

> "Talk, without effort, is nothing."
>
> —MARIA STEWART

When we know better (for children), we do better (for children).

I AM a disruptor of harm in the world and a kind truth-teller, and I belong to Sister Yolanda.

> "One must tell the truth in kindness and in love. That is the responsibility. How one receives it, is not on you, but them."
>
> —YOLANDA SEALEY-RUIZ

When there is resistance to truth and justice for youth, be kind, but tell the truth and tell justice for youth.

I AM a self-caregiver. I pause to laugh and dance, and I belong to Sister Maya.

> "My mission in life is not merely to survive, but to thrive; and to do so with some passion, some compassion, some humor, and some style."
>
> —MAYA ANGELOU

As an educator, (re)member to thrive, smile, heal, dance, and laugh. You carry genius and joy already within you.

Chapter 3 Reflection

Select one or more questions to engage in a freewrite.

- What are some reactions and reflections you have about the music, art, and text from Chapter 3?
- What ideas and passages stand out for you and why?
- What parts do you want to explore and learn about more?
- What parts of the educational system have helped you grow?
- What parts of the educational system are in need of water?
- What do you plan to do to unearth genius and joy?

Take some time to color this image.

PART II

Expanding Our Harvest: Putting Culturally and Historically Responsive Education Into Practice

CHAPTER 4

Redesigning Curriculum and Assessment

LAYERED PLAYLIST

Songs that inspire me about curriculum, assessment, and their humanizing potential. Play them as you read this chapter.

"Painter Song," Norah Jones

"Come Away With Me," Norah Jones

"Mona Lisa," Nat King Cole

"A Love Supreme, Pt. I— Acknowledgement," John Coltrane

"There's Something Special," Pharrell Williams

"Just a Cloud Away," Pharrell Williams

"Feeling Good," Nina Simone

"Somewhere Over the Rainbow," Israel "IZ" Kamakawiwo'ole

"I Can See Clearly Now," Johnny Nash

"Wonderful (Stevie Wonder Dedication)," India.Arie

Anti-Racism

Joy

Elevate

"I see how much responsibility you have as an artist. You are the reflection of our times. So whether you're a writer, a dancer, filmmaker, painter, or sculptor... you are reflecting the times that we live in, and after you're gone, all that is left is that reflection."

—BISA BUTLER

Dream Variations
by Langston Hughes

To fling my arms wide
In some place of the sun,
To whirl and to dance
Till the white day is done.
Then rest at cool evening
Beneath a tall tree
While night comes on gently,
    Dark like me—
That is my dream!

To fling my arms wide
In the face of the sun,
Dance! Whirl! Whirl!
Till the quick day is done.
Rest at pale evening . . .
A tall, slim tree . . .
Night coming tenderly
    Black like me.

Ascend

Equity

Genius

117

Unearthing Thought

1. How do you define curriculum?

2. What meanings and feelings come to mind when you think about assessment?

3. What creative steps do you take when writing or adapting lessons or unit plans?

4. How do you see the world as curriculum? When you walk about, what curriculum do you see on the earth? How might you connect it to your content area(s)?

5. Of all the things in the world, what must you teach?

6. Which curricular stories, topics, or teachings do you wish you had learned in your PreK–12 education?

7. How was your school's curriculum developed? Were teachers, parents, and young people involved?

8. What is a metaphor to represent the goals of curriculum, instruction, and assessment? Describe why you chose it.

9. How can we reimagine and redesign curriculum, instruction, and assessment?

10. What do you hope curriculum and assessment will accomplish?

(Re)defining Teacher as Artist and Curriculum as Artistry

When I seek to understand and create curriculum, I go to artists and artistry. Artists are special gifts because of the ways they "see" the unseen—the ways they express language and use their creative imaginations. They create beauty from the realms of the earth and cosmos that give true understandings in ways that other forms of communication may not. *Imagination* is a beautiful word that was used by the ancestors, and it is certainly one of the founts of joy. I am fascinated by artists' creative processes and sensibilities—by how they see the world as their muse and express the joys of creation and the social consciousness of pain and fatigue, sometimes all at once. Artists give us pathways of learning that do not feel rote or contrived, but instead organic and natural. Their teachings connect to our minds, hearts, spirits, and practice.

These are the very feelings and observations I experience when I create curriculum. It is an artistic process that enables me to share stories of the earth with students. Curriculum as a form of artistry was always at the center for Black ancestors. They used visual art, music, poetry, and other forms of creative expression in their teaching. Their art was culturally and historically responsive to the lives of people and to the social realities of the times. It became *our* curriculum and carried us through generations. For example, in the September 8, 1865, edition of *The Elevator*, a Black newspaper, the editor expressed the purpose and power of art to cultivate genius and joy (see the piece on the next page).

When I read and reread this piece, I am struck by the arts and the power they have to teach us and our children. While we wait for educational laws and mandates to embrace justice and equity, we must continue giving young people what they need to thrive in this world. As we continue to live in the world of strife, where mass shootings of our people, including our children, and other harms to humanity are commonplace, I am reminded of the power that curriculum holds for "the people"— for all humanity.

I begin each chapter with a layered playlist of "harmonious melodies" and weave visual art throughout the book not just to strengthen your understanding of my message, but also to model what we must do for our students. We need to share music, poetry, painting, and other forms of art with them regularly—for them to "listen to," "observe," and learn from. Such layering of multimodal and artistic texts, as the *Elevator* editor put it, provides "food for thought" and gives an example of what Black literary society members called "intellectual feasts." They used this term

The Fine Arts—Music, Painting and Poetry

"Let me write the songs for the people," said an ancient writer, "and I care not who makes the laws,"—intimating thereby that the hearts of "the people" were easier reached through the senses than through the judgment. And so it is even now as then. A love of the Arts, and an appreciation of the beautiful and true, is doing more to bring American people to a just realization of their duty than all the laws ever made, or all proclamations ever issued.

Within the past four years of war and strife, more true poetry has been written which sinks deep into the hearts of "the people," and there remains; more stirring music has been composed, which strikes the popular ear, and the strains become familiar, while harmonious melodies wake the mighty soul of "the people," and give it food for thought; more sublime conceptions have sprung from brain of the limner, and have been cut in stone, etched metal and portrayed on canvas, which delight the eye lead the public mind to higher and holier ideas of patriotism, than decades could produce under other circumstances.

The events of the times have given new inspiration to the poet, painter, and musician, and gloriously have they fulfilled their mission, which is "To wake the soul by tender strokes of Art; To raise the genius and to mend the heart."

Every loyal newspaper contains rich gems of poesy, which awaken in us new thoughts and loftier aspirations. Much of it poor and weak, emanating from the "callow poets" of the age; but much, also, evinces poetic genius.

It is music and painting which show the public feeling and lead the popular taste. They appeal directly to the senses, without an effort, while poetry requires the reflecting mind to appreciate it.

September 8, 1865 edition of *The Elevator*

The Fine Arts—Music, Painting and Poetry.

"Let me write the songs for the people," said an ancient writer, "and I care not who makes the laws,"—intimating thereby that the hearts of "the people" were easier reached through the senses than through the judgment. And so it is even now as then. A love of the Arts, and an appreciation of the beautiful and true, is doing more to bring the American people to a just realization of their duty than all the laws ever made, or all the proclamations ever issued.

Within the past four years of war and strife, more true poetry has been written which sinks deep into the hearts of "the people," and there remains; more stirring music has been composed, which strikes the popular ear, and the strains become familiar, while harmonious melodies wake the mi[...] it food[...] tions [...] limner[...] in me[...] deligh[...] to hig[...] than [...] circum[...]

The events of the times have given new inspiration to the poet, painter and musician, and gloriously have they fulfilled their mission, which is

"To wake the soul by tender strokes of Art; To raise the genius and to mend the heart."

Every loyal newspaper contains rich gems of poesy, which awaken in us new thoughts and loftier aspirations. Much of it poor and weak, emanating from the "callow poets" of the age; but much, also, evinces true poetic genius.

It is music and painting which show the public feeling and lead the popular taste. They appeal directly to the senses, without an effort, while poetry requires the reflecting mind to appreciate it. Still

to name what happened when they gathered to share words of truth and power. Their words provided nourishment and fulfillment.

"To wake the soul by tender strokes of Art; To raise the genius and to mend the heart," entices me to listen and learn, as this ancestor beautifully situates art (or curriculum) as the mechanisms to "wake the soul," "raise the genius," and "mend the heart." These are similar goals we must hold as educators in schools and classrooms but these must first be goals for ourselves.

Bisa Butler is a contemporary artist who carries on the pursuits of the ancestors and takes the responsibility of the artist seriously. She explains that artists' works are reflections of our times, which may include the past, present, and future. She stresses the permanence of our art (including curriculum), and how it leaves reflections, imprints, and legacies on the earth. Curriculum defined in this way can be (re)membered for decades to come. She says, *Whether you're a writer, a dancer, filmmaker, painter, or sculptor* (and I will add, teacher or educator), *you are reflecting the times*. Our curriculum and instruction allow us to be artists, and reflect on and respond to the social times. Years ago, as an English language arts educator, I stopped calling myself a writing teacher and started calling myself an English language *artist*, helping children to see language as art and beauty, as the title implies.

Seeing curriculum as a packaged, skills-only set of materials, textbooks, or state standards has been the traditional view. We tend to think of curriculum as something provided to teachers for teaching and learning. In some schools, teachers create their own curriculum, using state standards or expectations for learning across the content areas. Given the traditional problems with curricula (discussed in Chapter 1), I ask, *What could happen if we approached curriculum more artfully and more connected to the earth?* In the next section, I extend definitions of curriculum, while keeping in mind the teacher's role as beautiful and genius artist.

The World as Curriculum

Defining the world as curriculum means we must move about and navigate the world, and see it as full of opportunities for teaching and learning. Often, I ask teachers to take a walk across any landscape and describe what they see. *How can the people, places, lands, objects, animals, and things around them become ideas for teaching and learning?* For example, if you were to see a beautiful historic tree with striking buttress roots pushing up from the ground and interweaving with the soil and the trunk, what ideas for teaching and learning might come to mind?

Buttress roots are "aerial extensions of lateral surface roots and form only in certain species. Buttress roots stabilize the tree, especially in shallow saturated soils, thereby resisting toppling" (Oxford Dictionary of Biology, 2019).

I ask teachers and other developers of curriculum:

- What music and other sounds, paintings, and other visuals, digital creations, and so on do you see and feel? (Art)

- What language, writing, and metaphors do you see and feel? (English Language Arts)

- What examples of fitness and wellness do you see and feel? (Health and Physical Education)

- What representations of numbers, quantities, and space do you see and feel? (Mathematics)

- What branches of knowledge and discovery do you see and feel? (Science)

- What histories and contemporary realities do you see and feel? (Social Studies)

Their responses become ideas to bring into the classroom. My goal is to cultivate curriculum fluency among teachers, meaning the ability to look at anything around them quickly and develop curriculum from it. Just as I want children to develop reading fluency, I want teachers to develop curriculum fluency to come up with ideas expeditiously and with excellence.

Curriculum as Stories and Storytelling

Curriculum defined as stories and storytelling relates to the worthwhile narratives of humanity. Reading, telling, and listening to diverse stories are key to learning in school. We must ask whose stories have been told and taught (and from whose perspectives) and whose stories have not. Stories have a special quality of helping children to (re)member. They can be both real and imagined, and joy is connected to both types. As a reading specialist, I often give diagnostic assessments and find that students typically score higher on comprehension measures when they read narrative passages or texts, compared to informational passages or texts. That may be partly due to the power of stories to linger in our short-term and long-term memories. Stories provide a context for and connection to human lives.

I define curriculum as stories and storytelling because of their richness. I am not just referring to traditional literary themes and elements, such as characterization and plot, but the nuances, reflections, meanings, life lessons, and life connections to stories. Curriculum as stories and storytelling helps us to apply skills and standards to daily life. Importantly, artists across time have been creating and teaching through stories. For example, in Stevie Wonder's 1976 album, *Songs in the Key of Life*, each track tells a story. When I listen to it, I wonder, *What would curriculum in the key of life look and feel like for a child and teacher?*

The reason educational leaders police curriculum and create policies around anti-Blackness and anti-critical race theory is because they seek to control stories in the hearts and minds of children. Consequently, as they grow older, those children are likely to teach the same false, incomplete, or harmful narratives to their children. In this way, curriculum is generational. I wonder how those leaders must feel about themselves restraining complete, justice-centered stories in schools. I ask teachers and curriculum developers, *Which stories do schools consider worthwhile? What criteria were used to select those stories? How do the stories we teach elevate students' HILL (histories, identities, literacies, and liberation)?*

Curriculum as Legacy and Legacy Building

Curriculum defined as legacy and legacy building means that what we teach and how we teach it must leave an imprint on the lives of our students. It should feel special and enduring. Such curriculum should encourage and enable students to feel, and act toward improving the self and the world. What is being taught and learned should be significant, meaningful, and unique to our communities. Curriculum as legacy and legacy building should leave a stamp on our culture—and lead to a record of our times. Every time I develop a lesson, unit plan, or learning experience, I try to build in the legacies of the ancestors—this is what the five pursuits enable. I ask teachers and curriculum developers: *What legacies do you wish to create? What do you want to be known for? What imprints and trajectories do you want to make?*

These ways of (re)defining and (re)conceptualizing curriculum are dynamic and push boundaries of imaginings of who our students can become. Curriculum must not only connect to the world, but must also disrupt hurt, harm, and pain in the world. So, it's important to ask yourself, does my current curriculum:

- implicitly or explicitly contribute to others' hurt, harm, or pain?
- silence others' hurt, harm, or pain?
- actively disrupt others' hurt, harm, or pain, and bring joy?

We must question curriculum and the great impact it can have. Of course, curriculum should always connect to justice, equity, anti-racism, and other anti-oppressions, and the ultimate goal of curriculum should be joy.

The Creative Design of Curriculum

Given the extended definitions of curriculum I've presented thus far, and the five pursuits of identity, skills, intellect, criticality, and joy, educators often ask me, Where do I begin creating curriculum? After engaging in the self-work discussed in Chapter 3 and gaining knowledge about our students and communities, we are more prepared to move into pedagogy.

I begin the process by reflecting on the question, *Of all the stories, subjects, and topics in the world, which ones have you always wanted to teach?*

Depending on the moment in time, I answer this question differently. I often start by reading the world and thinking about the needs of our children—specifically, what they need to learn in the moment. At times, I start with a text I want to teach, a state standard my students need to learn, or a theme that addresses the needs of young people—a theme I know well and have a desire to teach. Children help me answer this question: *What do you want to learn about?* This question is important because the answers give us authentic purposes for teaching. We cannot teach themes, topics, or texts simply because they're in the "textbook" or "program." We must study curriculum to ensure that learning experiences reflect the needs and identities of our students.

From that question, I move into an artistic designer mode and take on the identity of a fashion/clothing designer. Clothing is very special. It covers us and protects our beautiful skin from toxins and injury. Clothing helps to define the social times we are living in and is one of the basic needs, one can argue, for humanity. It helps to define social image and identity. Historically, there are deep connections between clothing and diverse cultures around the world. Depending on the quality of the fabric, clothing feels good and looks good on us. The fabric is special, too, because its colors and patterns can spark joy and meaning. And, much like other artists, clothing designers develop their art for the world using a creative and expressive process. I've always been intrigued by fashion/clothing designers because they create beautiful garments from cloth (working from scratch or reworking existing garments). There are even designers who create fashion from materials that aren't typically used to make clothing, such as metal and plastic. But still, they use their tools, their gifts, to make others look and feel good.

The clothing designer's goal is similar to the curriculum developer's goal. Just as the clothing designer creates clothes to protect wearers and make them feel good and joyful, the curriculum designer creates curriculum to protect children and make them feel good and joyful.

I often compare curriculum to a ball gown. I wonder who sews the gown, just as I wonder who designs the curriculum that is given to teachers in schools. In Chapter 1, I discussed common problems with curriculum, followed by questions that we must ask ourselves about the curriculum that is placed in front of us. If we think of curriculum as a ball gown, we must be mindful that the hands that designed and created the gown are not always hands of color or sociopolitically conscious hands. Some who design curriculum for our classrooms have never been classroom teachers. And here is the gown, which appears beautiful, glorious, and

I often compare curriculum to a ball gown. I wonder who sews the gown, just as I wonder who designs the curriculum.

colorful. But I've learned throughout my career that everything that looks beautiful, glorious, and colorful at the onset is not always good for us, for our students, and for our futures.

And when the creation does not fit a child, we say things such as, "The child needs an intervention," and put the onus on the child and not the curriculum. Can you imagine if a designer created a gown for you, without your input, without learning about you, and when the day comes to try it on, it's too small—and you're told you need to go on a diet or gain weight? And you think, *But you never took my measurements.* That is what's happening in schools. Curriculum is being designed and implemented without taking the full measurements of our children. It is being designed and implemented in ways that do not connect to or reflect their lives and liberatory narratives of the world. We don't ask, what is the dress (or curriculum) for? So we try to manipulate the gown. We may cut off sleeves and other parts so children can fit into it, even though the gown was never designed for their bodies in the first place. So, I ask, How can curriculum be more excellently designed for the sake of all of our children and what they need to be elevated in this world?

A Step-by-Step Process for Designing Curriculum

Next, I present a step-by-step process for designing curriculum. As you read, I implore you to imagine you are the designers of curriculum and consider what it would take to create the best possible ball gown for our children.

Step 1: Get to Know Students

If you are designing a dress for someone you have yet to meet, what is the first thing you would do? You would likely introduce yourself and get to know the person— just as you likely do at the start of the year, when you build authentic and trusting relationships with students. You have to build trust with your students so that they trust you are the best instructor for them. Children need to trust that they have the best, brightest, and most conscious teacher in front of them. How does that trust happen? By getting to know our students in a variety of ways. The simplest way is by talking with them, engaging with them, and listening. But we can also get to know them through watching them interact with other children, observing them as they work and play, reading their writing, and other observational methods. And it's important that we not only get to know them, but that they get to know us. I've seen many teachers *keep themselves* from their students—including their interests, personalities, and what they love on earth. Children must know us and feel safe during our instruction.

Step 2: Assess Students Equitably

After getting to know students' histories and identities, the ways they use literacy in the world, the stories of their ancestors and their liberation, and their families and communities, the next step is to "take their measurements." Now, historically we have done that by determining their reading and math levels. But what happens when we expand the idea of measurement-taking to include equity, and culturally and historically responsive teaching and learning? We get a greater amount of data on children.

Below are some culturally and historically responsive assessment questions that you can ask students in small groups, individually, or in wide-scale surveys. They will help you gauge their understandings and needs of the pedagogy and where they are in terms of pursuing identity, skills, intellect, criticality, and joy. You can use the questions:

- as a diagnostic form of assessment to inform your instruction.
- as a benchmark form of assessment to determine the growth of children in the five pursuits at the beginning of the school year, middle of the year, and end of the year.
- as a pre- and post-assessment to see how your instruction throughout the school year or over a semester has impacted students' growth and achievement in these five core areas.
- to justify the need for culturally and historically responsive education by asking students, parents, and teachers, and then triangulating and comparing responses.

Keep in mind that the questions can be adapted to respond to the needs of your students, as well as their grade levels and age groups. I suggest selecting one to three questions from each pursuit. Questions are close-ended, open-ended, and short response, and some require a response on a numerical scale.

IDENTITY

1. Do you feel you have a voice in what you learn?
2. Do you feel valued in school?
3. How would you describe yourself to someone who doesn't know you?
4. What culture(s) do you identify with?
5. How would you describe yourself?
6. How would others describe you?
7. What can we do to help you feel better about being at school?
8. Is it important for you to be able to discuss race and identity at school?
9. Is it important to learn about yourself at school?
10. Is it important to learn about other people and different cultures?
11. What is one talent that a teacher didn't recognize in the past?
12. Do you have a strong sense of self? Do you know who you are and feel good about yourself?
13. Do you see yourself in other students' learning?
14. Do you take time to notice the beauty of differences in your class?
15. Do you feel you can be yourself in your school?

SKILLS

1. What is your favorite school subject?
2. Which school subject do you least like?
3. How do you learn best?
4. What skill(s) would like to learn this year, and why?
5. What are the projects or class activities that you have enjoyed most or felt most proud of? Can you describe what made them enjoyable?
6. When learning something new, what helps you?
7. Is it okay to get something wrong in class? Why?
8. What is something you learned to do? How did you learn it?
9. What are your strongest skills?
10. What skill(s) would you like to work on?
11. How do you know when you are doing well at school?
12. Do you know why you learn skills at school and how they apply to your future?
13. Are skills helping you to think or just to prepare for the test? Or both?
14. What is your strongest content area/school subject?
15. What is your most challenging content area/school subject?

INTELLECT

1. What topics do you want to learn about?
2. Are you learning things that are connected to life?
3. What are some issues in society that need change (to be better)?
4. Do you enjoy debating?
5. What type of person do you want to be when you get older, and how can the school help you to become that person?
6. Does your learning connect to the real world?
7. How does what you learn in school help you in the "real world"?
8. What have you learned at our school that is valuable and will help you be successful in life?
9. Does what you have learned help in other subject areas?
10. What has helped you become more engaged in learning?
11. What electives would benefit you most as a learner and leader?
12. If you can have a class about any topic, what would it be about?
13. Can you name a new person you learned about this year?
14. Do you learn about the other countries and parts of the world?
15. Is learning about new people, places, and things easy?

CRITICALITY

1. Would you like to learn about justice and how to make the world a better place?
2. Do you learn about fairness in school?
3. In what ways do current events going on in our country connect to your learning at school?
4. How often do you feel engaged in issues about justice in school?
5. Do you learn about justice, fairness, and equality at home?
6. Does our school offer opportunities to advocate for change—to make communities better?
7. Do you talk about race and justice in class?
8. Do you talk about race and justice at home?
9. What do you love about our community outside of school?
10. What would you change about our community outside of school?
11. How often do you have a voice in what you learn?
12. How would you like to make an impact on our community?
13. Do you feel safe and empowered?
14. Have you experienced an injustice? Was it resolved? If so, how?
15. Do you feel everyone is treated equally in the world?

JOY

1. Do you experience joy in our school?
2. How important is joy to you in school?
3. If you could create a program for kids, what would it be about?
4. Give an example when you felt joy at your school.
5. I think joy is _____.
6. How can you provide joy to your school and community?
7. Do you feel like you learn about beauty in the world?
8. Do you feel like you learn about the truth in history?
9. What is your favorite time of day in school?
10. What factors motivate you to learn?
11. What is one joyful experience you had last school year? Can you explain?
12. What brings you joy in the morning?
13. What brings you joy at the end of the day?
14. How can I make learning at school more joyful?
15. Do your teachers bring joy to your classroom?

Share data on student identity, skills, intellect, criticality, and joy with parents, community members, and school board members. I suspect they will be excited to read student data on joy.

Step 3: Draft the Curriculum Creatively

Once you have gotten to know the students and have equitable "measurements," you can begin to draft curriculum for them, using any sort of creative process or mechanisms that you like. Some teachers like to sketch out their creative ideas, while others like to write them down or use bullet points to capture their plans for teaching and learning. This step of drafting and sketching should be recursive and joyful, and you should share your ideas with students and their families for their input. Be sure to consider the five pursuits by asking yourself how the theme or topic (or the intellectual goal) could connect to 1) students' identities or the lives of others; 2) state standards or proficiencies; 3) intellect; 4) criticality; and 5) joy.

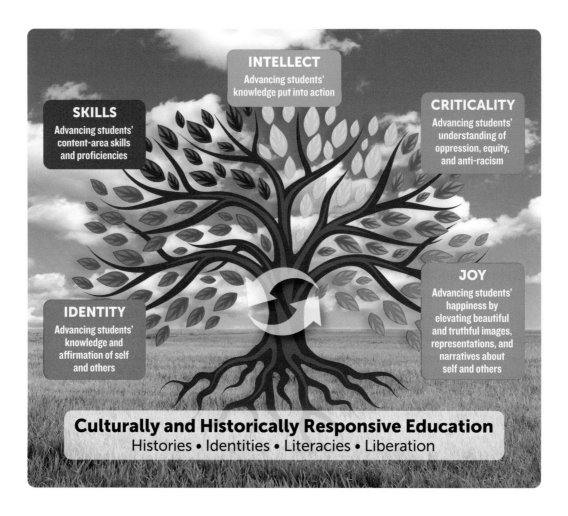

INTELLECT
Advancing students' knowledge put into action

SKILLS
Advancing students' content-area skills and proficiencies

CRITICALITY
Advancing students' understanding of oppression, equity, and anti-racism

IDENTITY
Advancing students' knowledge and affirmation of self and others

JOY
Advancing students' happiness by elevating beautiful and truthful images, representations, and narratives about self and others

Culturally and Historically Responsive Education
Histories • Identities • Literacies • Liberation

Step 4: Refine Your Design

Refine your design by thinking about the pacing of your lesson or unit plan, and the texts, supplies, and materials you'll need. For this step, I use a template for legacy unit plans. You will see, on the next page, examples of ways to address the pursuits, on the topic of Nelson Mandela and Apartheid, using the picture book *Nelson Mandela* by Kadir Nelson.

LEGACY UNIT PLAN, PART A

NAME(S) OF TEACHER(S) *the name(s) of the teacher(s) who created the unit plan*	**GRADE LEVEL(S)** *of the unit plan*
TOPIC OR THEME OF UNIT PLAN *the specific topic or theme that undergirds the learning*	**CONTENT AREA(S)** *of the unit plan*

TITLE OF UNIT PLAN *a creative title that reflects the topic or theme*
ESSENTIAL QUESTION(S) *essential (deep and thought-provoking) question(s) that will guide students' learning*
OVERVIEW OF UNIT PLAN *a 3–5 sentence summary/synthesis of the unit plan, which is useful for leaders who will support and observe parts of it*
TEACHERS' PRIOR KNOWLEDGE AND PRE-REFLECTION *any reflection and knowledge needed prior to teaching the unit plan*
STUDENTS' PRIOR KNOWLEDGE AND PRE-REFLECTION *any reflection and knowledge needed prior to learning within the unit plan*

LEGACY UNIT PLAN, PART B

CHRE TEACHING AND LEARNING PURSUITS

Add the pursuits, using common language. The most frequently used forms of pursuit-writing include:

I Can statements: This form is competency-based and puts goals in the voice of the student. Example: **Identity:** I can learn about South Africans of Color and make cultural connections to my own life. **Skills:** I can learn how to draw inferences and cite evidence from the text. **Intellect:** I can learn about the leadership and abolitionist work of Nelson Mandela. **Criticality:** I can learn about the Apartheid and the injustices inflicted upon Black and Brown people. **Joy:** I can learn about the joy of South Africans and the importance of starting with their genius and joy.	**1. Identity:** **2. Skills:** State Standard(s): **3. Intellect:** **4. Criticality:** **5. Joy:**
Students Will (be able to) statements: This is the most traditional form. Because the verb "learn" is general, it could be replaced with more specific verbs. Example: **Identity:** Students will learn about South Africans of Color and make cultural connections to their own lives. **Skills:** Students will learn how to draw inferences and cite evidence from the text. **Intellect:** Students will learn about the leadership and abolitionist work of Nelson Mandela. **Criticality:** Students will learn about Apartheid and the injustices inflicted upon Black and Brown people. **Joy:** Students will learn about the joy of South Africans and the importance of starting their stories with their genius and joy.	**1. Identity:** **2. Skills:** State Standard(s): **3. Intellect:** **4. Criticality:** **5. Joy:**

Questions: This form is inquiry-based because you come up with questions that students answer. Example:

Identity: Who are South Africans of Color, and what cultural connections can I make to my own life?

Skills: How do I draw inferences and cite evidence from the text?

Intellect: Who was Nelson Mandela, and what made his leadership and abolitionist work important?

Criticality: What was Apartheid, and what were the injustices inflicted upon Black and Brown people?

Joy: In what ways is the South African culture genius and beautiful?

1. Identity:

2. Skills:

State Standard(s):

3. Intellect:

4. Criticality:

5. Joy:

ASSESSMENT

Determine how each pursuit will be assessed. Example:

Identity: Students will learn about South Africans of Color and make cultural connections to their own lives.
(Assessment: Students will create a poster or digital video of the genius and joy of South Africans detailing what they learned about them and the similarities they found in their own lives.)

Skills: Students will learn to draw inferences and cite evidence from the text.
(Assessment: Students will independently read text and respond to tasks.)

Intellect: Students will learn about the leadership and abolitionist work of Nelson Mandela.
(Assessment: Students will recall what they learned about Mandela on a formative assessment exit ticket or worksheet.)

Criticality: Students will learn about Apartheid and the injustices inflicted toward Black and Brown people.
(Assessment: Students will recall what they learned about Apartheid on a formative assessment exit ticket or worksheet.)

Joy: Students will learn about the joy of South Africans and the importance of starting a story with their genius and joy.
(Assessment: Students will create a poster or digital video of the genius and joy of South Africans detailing what they learned about them.)

LEGACY UNIT PLAN, PART C

TEXT SELECTION
List of the multimodal, diverse texts that will be used during the unit. The anchor text is the main or central reading, which may be a textbook, novel, picture book, or other form of text. Layered texts should support the anchor text and be short and powerful.

- Anchor Text:
- Layered Texts:

FAMILY/HOME CONNECTION
What families and caregivers can do (or answer) together to support learning.

MISCONCEPTIONS
Any misconceptions related to the unit's topic or theme that will be addressed in truthful ways. Addressing misconceptions helps to clarify falsehoods, stereotypes, and misunderstandings.

SOCIAL-EMOTIONAL LEARNING
Standards or questions that address students' social-emotional needs, focusing on self-awareness, relationship-building, feelings, anti-trauma, and positive thinking and living.

LEGACY UNIT PLAN, PART D

STUDENT SPARK *Ways teacher(s) will open the unit to create engagement and interest in the theme and topic.*	
UNIT BREAKDOWN *Details and description of the unit's breakdown by weeks or days in sequence of teaching and learning. Consider labeling which pursuit(s) are addressed during specific weeks or days. This requires being mindful of strategies, methods, differentiation, accommodations, and approaches to teaching and learning that are specific and research-based.*	
SOCIAL ACTION EXTENSION *An idea of how students will connect learning to social action to combat inequities in their local or wider community. This can be a culminating project.*	

When planning, resist shallow levels of culturally responsive teaching, and instead, focus on full implementation of the five pursuits. The goal is to plan for and reach Level III.

Level I Culturally Responsive Teaching and Learning: Multicultural Representation Only. There is deep knowing, teaching, discussion, or assessment of identities, culture, or race, but perhaps only some knowledge of children's identities and cultures by the teacher.

Level II Culturally Responsive Teaching and Learning: Multicultural Representation + Knowing, Affirming and Celebrating Children's Identities, Cultures, and Races. Children experience learning activities connected to academics, identity development, and sociopolitical consciousness, but no learning objectives or assessments are set or enacted.

Level III Culturally Responsive Teaching and Learning: Multicultural Representation + Knowing, Affirming and Celebrating Children's Identities, Cultures, and Races Deeply + CHRE/five pursuits in teaching, learning, and assessment.

Step 5: Choose Multimodal Texts

Select quality, multimodal texts that support learning—or, metaphorically, the fabric of the dress (and fabric matters!). Multimodal texts are visual, auditory, and other sensory texts layered upon the central or anchor text of the learning. Layers of text add significantly to the meaning and comprehension of student understanding (Muhammad, 2020). We need quality, multicultural, and multimodal text selection. A dress can have a beautiful design, but if the fabric is of poor quality, it can cheapen the final product. When designing curriculum, the texts we select must be high quality. They must be interesting and complex, while speaking to students' multiple identities and needs. For each pursuit, choose supportive layered texts. I recommend going beyond traditional texts by including artwork, speeches, picture books, primary source documents, infographics, TED Talks, podcasts, images, performances, short films and other types of films, maps, social media (such as memes, short clips, and posts), real-life objects, quotations, and any other types of texts that you can imagine. Texts are anything we can read and make meaning from, so don't only think of books and other forms of print. Think of oral histories, traditions, and social context as texts, too.

Children often disengage from learning because the texts we give them don't speak to their lives, including their cultural identities, interests, histories, and experiences. They may find the texts to be meaningless or irrelevant to their lives. So, it is important to make connections through texts, to their identities, interests, histories, and experiences. It is also important to give children texts by diverse authors and in a variety of modes on topics that don't always connect directly to our disciplines. For example, we can bring psychology-related texts to English language arts, sociology-related texts to mathematics, or business texts to science. When we diversify the modes, we also diversify the levels of learning.

Also, think about format. For example, if a child struggles reading print texts, consider giving that child a video or audio text at a higher comprehension level. A child's listening comprehension may be slightly higher than her or his individual print-reading comprehension. Texts should also center justice and joy so students see beautiful manifestations of who they are, who they were (their people), and who they can become.

Step 6: Make Final Modifications
Finishing your curricular design involves making final modifications to your lesson or unit plan and the story you're teaching. Ultimately, you want all the parts of the lesson or unit plan to connect. This can be done individually or in collaboration with fellow genius educators.

Step 7: Teach and Adjust
Finally, you are ready for the "fitting"—to try the dress on the person for whom you created it. In other words, it is time to teach the lesson or parts of the unit plan. And while you do that, you'll likely make adjustments along the way. And just as a designer would make adjustments while the dress is still on the person, we need to make adjustments to our lesson or unit plan in real time, while teaching and observing children and their reactions and responses to the learning.

Step 8: Apply Adjustments
When the teaching is complete, you can make further adjustments to get the fit just right. If you've created a true legacy unit plan, children this year, next year, and the years that follow will experience the same high level of learning.

Step 9: Assess the Curriculum With Students
We return to who we are creating the dress for, or the curriculum for and assess how it fit and made the wearer feel. What follows are questions you can ask individual students, small groups of students, or the whole class, after you've taught the unit plan. Be sure to integrate findings from your initial round of assessment questions (pp. 127–129) with your findings from this round.

- How did the unit help you learn something about yourself or others? What did you learn? How can that knowledge help you in life now? In the future?

- How do you feel about the new content skills you learned in this unit? Do you feel a sense of achievement and independence when you apply the skills?

- How do you feel about the new knowledge gained from this unit? How can that knowledge help you in life now? In the future?

- How do you feel about the learning related to equity, power, and social justice? How can that knowledge help you in life now? In the future?

- How do you feel about learning related to joy? How can that knowledge help you in life now? In the future?

Step 10: Reflect on Yourself as a Professional

This step involves post-reflection on how the unit progressed. You would reflect on your own professionalism and qualities as a pedagogue. You might also invite critique on ways to improve and advance your practice. One thing I like most about watching *Project Runway,* a television show about the artistic design and creation of clothing, is the critique at the end of each episode. Imagine what would happen if our unit plans were critiqued in ways that only help us to improve and advance our practice. I wonder whether it is easy to accept critique on something special, like our artwork, or curriculum. *How will we use comments to strengthen our curricular fluency and ability to design and implement curriculum?* If your unit plan was put in front of a panel of experts for funding and support, how would the panel respond? If children were on that panel to select from multiple unit plans, would they select yours?

This is also the step where you celebrate—where you experience the joy of completing something special that will, hopefully, leave a positive imprint on the thinking and lives of students.

The HILL Model can be adjusted, depending on how it is used in schools and classrooms (see Chapters 5 and 6). When the model is used in a lesson or unit plan, it is important to keep in mind that the pursuits were not designed to be taught each day, but across the weeks of the unit or the days of the lesson. It is also important to know that if you are not practicing and performing well in the pursuits named in the lesson or unit, it will be quite difficult to teach them and to engage students and help them achieve. And finally, remember that the pursuits are just goals for learning that help us to outline and frame our practices. You still need excellent strategies and methods to teach the pursuits well.

Keep in mind that the pursuits were not designed to be taught each day, but across the weeks of the unit or the days of the lesson.

I just walked you through a step-by-step process for designing curriculum from scratch. But the truth of the matter is you could take an existing curriculum, just like an existing dress, and adapt it to make it culturally and historically responsive, folding in the five pursuits and using layered texts. Either approach is curricular progress, especially if you've been focusing mainly on skills.

Assessing the CHRE Pursuits

During the first year in my teacher education program, I learned a very useful definition of assessment. I learned that "to assess" means "to gather information." Often, assessment is equated with just grading, assigning points, or giving formal letter grades. Culturally and historically responsive assessment keeps the foundations of equity, justice, genius, and joy at the core, while encouraging us to understand how children are experiencing the learning and performing across the five pursuits. Everything we teach across the five pursuits should be assessed.

Strong assessment means that students are somehow involved in the process. This can be as simple as giving them options on how they are assessed in each pursuit. Strong assessment should also advance learning and help us to reflect on our own performance as teachers—helping us to determine where we are strong and where we need more work. It should also reveal the genius of students, as well as areas where they need more support.

Culturally and historically responsive assessment must be interesting, multimodal, and creative, just as our instructional practices should be. It should show us the direction we need to go next in our teaching, and it should be reliable.

When I ask teachers what feelings or emotions come to mind when they think about assessment, many go straight to ones connected to standardized state exams, which have been written, designed, and formatted the same way for decades. In general, states and districts have not developed creative models or modes of student assessment, nor have standardized state exams assessed anything but state standards. At district and school levels, we rarely see widescale assessments related to identity, criticality, and joy. So, as with many other parts of the educational system, we must disrupt and reframe assessment.

An Example

In this section, I walk you through a process of creating culturally and historically responsive assessments, based on the five pursuits, for a unit on sugar. I start with writing a goal for the pursuit of intellect (Students will learn the origins of sugar and where it is grown) and move to identity, skills, criticality, and joy.

CHRE Pursuits

1. **Identity:** Students will record and analyze their daily sugar intake and compare it to normed nutrition-related data.

2. **Skills (Science and Disciplinary Literacy):** Students will conduct an experiment to learn about the sugar molecule and sucrose, and learn how to dissolve sugar.

   Disciplinary Literacy Skills: Students will learn to read and write a lab report.

3. **Intellect:** Students will learn the origins of sugar and where it is grown.

4. **Criticality:** Students will learn the harmful effects to the body of eating too much processed sugar.

5. **Joy:** Students will learn the benefits to the body of eating natural sugar.

Anchor Texts: Lab Report and Science Textbook

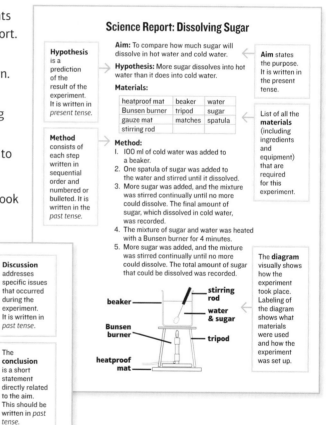

Science Report: Dissolving Sugar

Hypothesis is a prediction of the result of the experiment. It is written in *present tense.*

Aim: To compare how much sugar will dissolve in hot water and cold water.

Aim states the purpose. It is written in the present tense.

Hypothesis: More sugar dissolves into hot water than it does into cold water.

Materials:

heatproof mat	beaker	water
Bunsen burner	tripod	sugar
gauze mat	matches	spatula
stirring rod		

List of all the **materials** (including ingredients and equipment) that are required for this experiment.

Method consists of each step written in sequential order and numbered or bulleted. It is written in the *past tense.*

Method:
1. 100 ml of cold water was added to a beaker.
2. One spatula of sugar was added to the water and stirred until it dissolved.
3. More sugar was added, and the mixture was stirred continually until no more could dissolve. The final amount of sugar, which dissolved in cold water, was recorded.
4. The mixture of sugar and water was heated with a Bunsen burner for 4 minutes.
5. More sugar was added, and the mixture was stirred continually until no more could dissolve. The total amount of sugar that could be dissolved was recorded.

The **diagram** visually shows how the experiment took place. Labeling of the diagram shows what materials were used and how the experiment was set up.

beaker — stirring rod — water & sugar — Bunsen burner — tripod — heatproof mat

Results are usually presented in a table format. It is a recording of what was observed or measured during the experiment

Results:

Water	Dissolved Sugar (spatulas)
Cold	2
Hot	6

Discussion: More sugar dissolved in the hot water than in the cold water. A thermometer could have been used to measure the temperature of the water. The amount of sugar could have been measured more accurately by adding a smaller amount at a time.

Conclusion: Three times as much sugar dissolves in hot water as in cold water.

Discussion addresses specific issues that occurred during the experiment. It is written in *past tense.*

The **conclusion** is a short statement directly related to the aim. This should be written in *past tense.*

Layered Texts for a Unit on Sugar

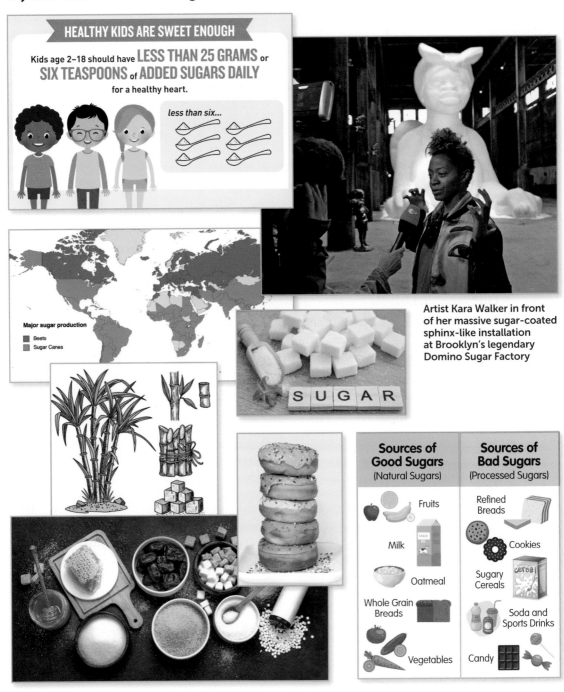

HEALTHY KIDS ARE SWEET ENOUGH

Kids age 2–18 should have **LESS THAN 25 GRAMS** or **SIX TEASPOONS** of **ADDED SUGARS DAILY** for a healthy heart.

less than six...

Major sugar production
- Beets
- Sugar Canes

SUGAR

Artist Kara Walker in front of her massive sugar-coated sphinx-like installation at Brooklyn's legendary Domino Sugar Factory

Sources of Good Sugars (Natural Sugars)	Sources of Bad Sugars (Processed Sugars)
Fruits	Refined Breads
Milk	Cookies
Oatmeal	Sugary Cereals
Whole Grain Breads	Soda and Sports Drinks
Vegetables	Candy

Assessments for the Unit

For this science unit, I give various types of assessments to provide students multiple opportunities for success. If I gave them just one summative quiz or test to assess all five pursuits, I would not give them a way to showcase their genius in its entirety. I open the unit with the intellect and skills pursuits in mind, although it's okay to open a unit with any of the five pursuits. I give homework related to the identity pursuit, and might extend the unit with projects, which I could use to assess all five pursuits.

1. **Identity:** Students will record and analyze their daily sugar intake and compare it to normed nutrition-related data. (Assessment: data-collection tool worksheet)

2. **Skills (Science and Disciplinary Literacy):** Students will conduct an experiment to learn about the sugar molecule and sucrose, and learn how to dissolve sugar. Disciplinary Literacy: Students will learn to read and write a lab report. (Assessment: group lab report, quiz)

3. **Intellect:** Students will learn the origins of sugar and where it is grown. (Assessment: quiz)

4. **Criticality:** Students will learn the harmful effects to the body of eating too much processed sugar. (Assessment: digital/video, poster, or written piece with compare and contrast of types of sugar)

5. **Joy:** Students will learn the benefits to the body of eating natural sugar. (Assessment: digital/video, poster, or written piece with compare and contrast of types of sugar)

Curriculum as Positive Light

> "You have a responsibility to educate your people, you have a responsibility to have your people shown in a positive light."
>
> —BISA BUTLER

I opened this chapter with a piece from the September 8, 1865, edition of *The Elevator*, in which the editor used the phrase "the people" repeatedly. That phrase reminded me that we are not only educating the children in front of us, but others as well. When we educate one child, we educate "the people," our people and future generations of those on the earth. Bisa Butler says we have a responsibility to our children, which in turn speaks to the responsibility we have to humanity. That responsibility includes the curriculum and instruction we put in front of children. It includes ensuring that our lessons, unit plans, and other learning experiences with children create a positive light and joy that permeates their lives. If joy is the ultimate goal of our teaching and learning, we must be sure children have positive learning experiences. I encourage you as I encourage myself to be the artist. Be the designer. Be the teacher. Certainly, we must be the genius and joy that our children need.

Chapter 4 Reflection

Select one or more questions to engage in a freewrite.

- What are some reactions and reflections you have about the music, art, and text from Chapter 4?
- What ideas and passages stand out for you and why?
- What parts do you want to explore and learn about more?
- What parts of the educational system have helped you to grow?
- What parts of the educational system are in need of water?
- What do you plan to do to unearth genius and joy?

Take some time to color this image.

CHAPTER 5

Practical and Creative Uses of the HILL Model:

Students, Teachers, and Staff Members

LAYERED PLAYLIST

Songs that inspire me about caring school communities. Play them as you read this chapter.

"Harvest for the World," The Isley Brothers

"Get Up, Stand Up," Bob Marley & the Wailers

"Freedom," Pharrell Williams

"Everybody Loves the Sunshine," Roy Ayers Ubiquity

"Water," Beyoncé, Pharrell Williams, and Salatiel

"Keep Your Head to the Sky," Earth, Wind & Fire

"Lovely Day," Bill Withers

"A Place in the Sun," Stevie Wonder

"Think," Aretha Franklin

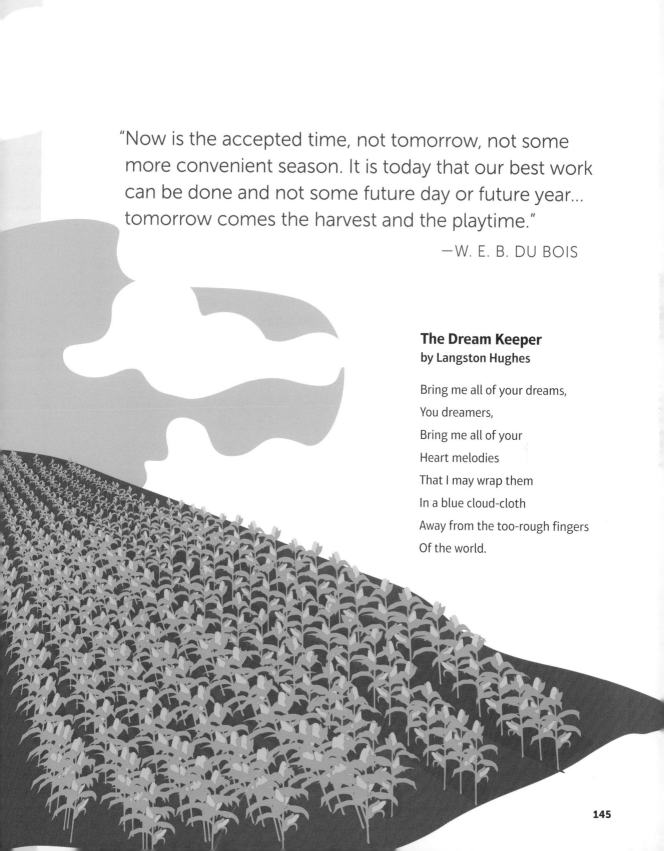

"Now is the accepted time, not tomorrow, not some more convenient season. It is today that our best work can be done and not some future day or future year... tomorrow comes the harvest and the playtime."

—W. E. B. DU BOIS

The Dream Keeper
by Langston Hughes

Bring me all of your dreams,
You dreamers,
Bring me all of your
Heart melodies
That I may wrap them
In a blue cloud-cloth
Away from the too-rough fingers
Of the world.

Unearthing Thought

1. How can the HILL Model best be used in your learning space?

2. How confident are you in your understanding of each pursuit and why?

3. How do you plan to start implementing the HILL model?

4. Which pursuits are new to you, and which are you already using in your instruction?

5. In which pursuits do you feel your students already excel, and in which do they need more support?

6. What new and creative ideas do you have for enacting the five pursuits?

7. When coming up with curricular ideas, what feelings and emotions do you experience?

8. What creative texts can you bring into teaching and learning that would help you carry out your ideas?

9. Will you begin adapting an existing lesson or unit in your curriculum or creating something new altogether?

10. Do you work most creatively alone or in collaboration with others?

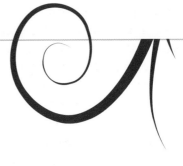

Creating Spaces for Genius and Joy

Harvest is a beautiful word because it connects to the earth. It means gathering substances from the rich earth that are needed to move forth life. A harvest redefines the word *richness* from gaining financial wealth and affluence to contributing to humanity and making the self and the world better. Harvest brings success, and not just success as in recognition and awards, but also success as in the feeling of beloved-ness when we contribute to making the world better. I consider all the beautiful, creative ideas and experiences we have with children in and around schools. It feels to me like a harvest of genius and joy. When educators ask me where to start with the five pursuits, I respond, "Bring teachers together and give them time and intellectual space to create curricular ideas. Give them a topic, theme, or idea and ask them to create learning experiences inspired by it." Often, when I work with teachers, I ask them to take an object at arm's length on their desk and create a lesson or unit plan that addresses each of the pursuits in connection to the object. At first, they are perplexed, but then ideas inevitably start flowing. Here are a few examples:

- **In front of me is a cup of coffee.** I can teach students about people who cultivate and harvest coffee beans (*Identity*); the physics or chemistry of coffee using the scientific method (science *Skills*); locations where coffee is grown across the world (*Intellect*); the extent to which financial wealth is returned to communities of color that cultivate and harvest coffee (*Criticality*); and the link between coffee (when consumed in moderation) and stronger cognitive functions and a more positive mood (*Joy*). Layered texts could include articles, maps, videos, visuals of process of cultivation, photographs, data charts, and scientific reports.

- **In front of me is an ink pen.** I can teach students how to use their pens to define who they are in writing (*Identity*), or to identify and compare themes of letter writing across diverse writers and parts of a letter (English language arts and social studies *Skills*). They can learn the history of letter writing across diverse communities (*Intellect*) and the ways we use letters for social change (*Criticality*). During the lesson or unit, students can write letters to themselves to boost their self-esteem or to a loved one (*Joy*). Layered texts could include letters, primary source documents, images of diverse tools for writing, and nonfiction essays.

- **In front of me is a Batman plush toy.** I can encourage students to talk or write about characters they love and/or relate to in the media or literature (*Identity*). They can research the number of readers and viewers of DC Comics and Marvel, calculate percentages, and compare them (*math Skills*). They can learn about the original and current purposes of comic books (*Intellect*). They can consider the historical representation and exclusion of people in comics based on ability, race, gender, religion, culture, age, sexuality, and other identities (*Criticality*). Lastly, they can consider how comics can help children and adults identify who they are and envision a better future (*Joy*). Layered texts could include comics from the past and present, videos, movie clips, images of characters, statistical charts, and infographics.

Here are other desk objects I've seen that have started a flow of ideas:

- index cards (engineering and building)
- beverage thermos (insulation, thermodynamics, and physics)
- stapler (simple machines)
- lamp (light, physics, microwaves, infrared, visible light, ultraviolet, and gamma rays)
- smartphone (communication, technology, and apps)
- keyboard (history of QWERTY and placement of keys or history of technology)
- plant (science of growing vegetation from soil and seeds)
- speaker (music history and culture)
- trail mix (walking, exercise, healthy nutrition)

The list goes on and on. As teachers' curricular fluency increased, they began to move faster to create pursuits around ideas because they were (and working to become) scholars of their disciplines. They became more aware of the histories of their disciplines, as well as related research, current events, and technologies. They began to see their content knowledge and skills in almost anything, from the objects on their desks to anything else in the world. A teacher at Yellowhab School in Virginia, Becky Schnekser, for example, said she wanted to use a cardboard box to teach math to her elementary students, and asked me how I would relate it as text to the HILL Model (histories, identities, literacies, and liberation). In the next five minutes, we constructed foundational pursuits for a unit plan and then created the full unit including the pedagogical methods and practices. The initial plan looked like this, with a connection to language arts and mathematics:

Identity: Students will consider the special items that they keep—items that help to restore and sustain who they are.

Skill: Students will learn about dimensions, shapes, and measurements. (Math)

Students will compose literary fiction involving keepsakes. (English Language Arts)

Intellect: Students will learn about cultural boxes and keepsakes, such as the Hope Chest.

Criticality: Students will learn how humans across time have moved, settled, and escaped for safety—seeking ways to preserve their culture and cultural artifacts.

Joy: Students will research artifacts their families have preserved that have brought personal fulfillment.

If we can create rich learning experiences from desk objects and a box, imagine what we can create when we see the world as our curricular muse and involve students and colleagues. Imagine the fun and joy. We will see something unique and beautiful emerge.

For that to happen, though, we must disrupt traditional, ineffective notions of schools and schooling. If you have colleagues who feel the model is "impossible," they are likely wed to traditional purposes for curriculum and instruction. But when we connect our minds and theirs to historical forms of excellence, it disrupts the norms we have come to know.

The HILL Model helps students put content skills into action at school, beyond school, and eventually in their work as adults. Not all children will grow up to be scientists, historians, writers, artists, athletes, or mathematicians, but they will hold jobs in which the five pursuits will be essential, and they'll need to see how they are situated and can be applied in a multitude of ways. All we need now is time to be creative with the model. In a stronger and more advanced educational system, teachers would have time to create and build genius and joy for themselves and students. In the following sections, I showcase various manifestations of the HILL Model to give you ideas to get started or continue your journey. I fully anticipate you will use your creativity to extend the ideas and dream up more ways the model can be used.

Not all children will grow up to be scientists, historians, writers, artists, athletes, or mathematicians, but they will hold jobs in which the five pursuits will be essential.

10 Creative Ways to Use the HILL Model

The HILL Model can be mandated, adopted, suggested, and encouraged across any school or district. It can also be used to teach any program or curriculum. Although it is mostly used for classroom instruction, it can also be used throughout a school or district for leaders and support staff to create a culturally and historically responsive environment. Here are 10 ways I've seen the model used to engage students, teachers, and staff, organized into three sections: Professional Learning, Approaches to Curriculum and Instruction, and Post-Instruction.

Professional Learning

1. Engage in Literary Societies or Book Clubs of Professional Materials

When we gather as professionals to build knowledge, we elevate our practice. So, I encourage you to engage in a literary society or book club in which you and your colleagues discuss professional resources for educators. With the surge of multimodal texts, your initiative doesn't have to center a print book; it could instead center a digital text, research or news article, podcast, video, film, primary source document, collection of social media posts, artwork, poetry, literary fiction, music lyrics, or another type of text that will help to shape your thinking and practice. We must (re)member that we don't just learn through traditional professional books, but through a wealth of resources. One reason I've layered Langston Hughes's poetry into this book is because he advances my thinking about humanity and what I need to do to be a better teacher. Whether you "read" or "view" the text depends on how much time you have to devote to the society or club.

Teachers don't always have to engage in "traditional book clubs" in which they meet to discuss ideas from the text and how they relate to or diverge from their own practices. Instead, teachers may also create their own "literary society," honoring the ways ancestors have gathered to cultivate literacies and learning historically. I have found that what made literary societies unique was:

- Naming the meetings "intellectual feasts."
- Crafting a preamble that states members' purposes for teaching and leading children.
- Establishing a library, resources, and booklists. As new societies are created, members should have access to the libraries, resources, and booklists of societies that came before them. These texts should be maintained and advanced each year.

- Meeting in a variety of rooms and other spaces.
- Reading diverse texts by diverse authors (including texts by members themselves).
- Cultivating the five pursuits to practice in their personal and professional lives.
- Inviting in young people and community members.
- Speaking truths and writing regularly.
- Engaging in a range of literacies (thinking, reading, writing, speaking, listening, and communication).
- Comparing members' learning with the current state of the world.
- Learning about oppression and joy.
- Creating platforms, such as newspapers, to share learnings with the world.

Consider organizing not only with immediate colleagues, but also with teachers across the world. After all, during the COVID-19 pandemic, we all embraced virtual forms of teaching and learning, which allowed us to engage with and learn from scholars almost anywhere and everywhere—and we got good at it. Also, when thinking about "membership," don't rule out young people, staff members, parents, professors, and other partners who would love to contribute and who might benefit from organized time to read, think, and reflect. Lastly, think about size. Do you want a smaller collective or a larger one?

Once your literary society is established, determine a name for it. The right name matters because it sends a message about who you are. You may choose something simple, such as Literary Society of _____ School, or you could choose a "catchy" name that suggest what you stand for such as the Genius and Joy Collective (GJC).

From there, choose a text, read or view it, and engage in thinking and learning. The HILL Model can be used as a basis for reflection questions for self-reflection, small-group discussion, or written response.

> **Identity:** How did this text help me to learn about or change something about myself, my thinking, my actions, or my professional identity as an educator? What did the text affirm about my teaching style and practices? How did the text (re)shape my racial, gender, cultural or other identities? What did I learn about cultural identities other than my own? How can this text further shape and refine my identities and sense of self and others?

Skills: What new pedagogical methods and skills did I learn about, and what do I want to try? How can this text further shape and refine my skills?

Intellect: What new people, places, concepts, laws, histories, and so on, did I learn? How does that new knowledge compare to what I already know? Have I learned something new that makes me want to disrupt an existing schema? How can this text further shape and refine my intellect?

Criticality: How did this text help me to understand my own biases, "-isms," or deficit thinking? How did it help me understand those of others? How did this text help me to understand systemic and structural racism and oppression? How will it enable me to bring more criticality into my content areas? How can this text further shape and refine my criticality?

Joy: How did this text help me to claim my joy and bring more joy into the classroom?

If you're reading a shorter text, such as a poem or song lyrics, come together and create specific discussion questions around the piece's language. For example, for the "Cultivating Genius Anthem" by 80's Babies, you could read and study the lyrics, which appear on page 153, and listen to the song to prepare questions.

Listen to "Cultivating Genius Anthem," with lyrics on the following page

Discussion Questions

- What does this song say about Black people and the genius within the culture? (*Identity*)

- What do you notice about the piece's language and messages? Select a line and describe its meaning. (*Skills*)

- How do we "develop intellectuals" in schools? (*Intellect*)

- How have systemic norms impeded growth of schools? What are some examples? (*Criticality*)

- What does the following line mean? *The genius lives inside of you, it's time for you to bring it out.* What is an example of your genius? (*Joy*).

After meeting, the group could engage in a social action project, where members create something or do something that contributes to the community.

"Cultivating Genius Anthem" by 80's Babies

Yeah. It's gon take us

To save us

I came to bare it all

So no make up or favors,

Do it on our own

Son we major we came up,

From the ground nobody make a move

Nobody make a sound it's going down,

Waiting on more blessings

They forgot too soon,

Time to celebrate,

Cuz believers come to spot the moon,

Step into the room

It's time to get active,

And let 'em all know that

Black is Attractive

We just want control

Like Damita Jo

Teaching all our kids what they need to know,

Waited long for the freedom song

You can sing it now,

The genius lives inside of you

It's time for you to bring it out,

Never spewing nonsense

This is culturally responsive,

Work so let it work and stop

Working against the progress,

Keep the kids first

Bring water when they thirst,

Do everything with love

But sometimes it might hurt,

Some talking equality

They saying it can't work,

But they don't quite understand

This equity framework,

And they don't understand

My spirit they can't hurt,

And when we spread the truth

We'll see who's in danger,

Cuz the leaders of the world

They look just like me,

And history gon back me up

I got all receipts,

As a child kinda wild

Could barely crawl I had to bring it,

Knew I wanted to fly

So I guess I had to wing it,

("If you're not inspired, you can't be human" —Pharrell Williams)

And this is not a start up

We write with permanent marker, you can't erase me

Cuz this story I'm the author,

Plant the seed made a tree

I'm the mother and the father,

Branched out through the hood

And developed young scholars,

Cultivate the skills

Teach em bout identity,

Develop intellectuals

And joy that's the energy,

Critical criticality never forget the lessons,

I understand my power

That's why I'm fighting oppression,

Fed up but don't confuse

My passion with aggression,

Gave y'all a pass

But y'all wanna keep testing,

Nooooo

So now you still fail,

If we keeping love first

You know the righteous will prevail,

Hats off to you

So you know I ain't capping,

They teaching our kids

The slave trade never happened,

That's why I'm educating

Most y'all just hear rappin,

But this is our culture turn it up

Let's blast it,

Now we gon come together they can't lie to me,

New school Black literary society,

No more forgotten readers

No more forgotten feeders,

No more of his-story

In the books for knowledge seekers,

We need something that is real,

Something tangible

We need something we can feel,

We need to elevate

That's why we headed up the HILL

We need to elevate

That's why we headed up the HILL (Pedagogies)

2. Check in With Students Through Questions, Conversations, and Critical Listening

Another way to use the HILL Model is through check-in questions, conversations, and critical listening with students. If you are not prepared to move to full lesson or unit planning, this is a good place to start to see how students are feeling about and reacting to classroom instruction, as well as how they're doing socially and emotionally. Though this strategy of "check-ins" involves informal conversations, student responses to the questions can inform our practices. Ask children questions, such as the ones that follow, throughout the school day to check in with them and their well-being.

Identity: How's your heart? How are you feeling today? What emotions are you feeling? How do you see yourself recognized in our school and classroom? How do you feel about yourself? How are you learning more about yourself and who you wish to be?

Skills: How do you feel about skills you've learned in our class? In what areas do you need more support? In what areas could you support a classmate?

Intellect: What topics or concepts would you like to learn more about? What do you think about the knowledge you have been cultivating in class?

Criticality: How are you reading the world? What are you noticing about what is happening in the world today and how it relates to what we learn in class?

Joy: How's your joy? What has brought you joy today or recently?

We ask what we value. When students see us engaged in more than just skills or state standards or state tests, they begin to value education more widely. In turn, I hope they feel safe, loved, and embraced by others. The model helps us to listen critically to students' experiences—and they need to be heard.

Approaches to Curriculum and Instruction

3. Take Time to Review and Evaluate Curriculum

Before adapting school curriculum, take time to review and evaluate how culturally and historically responsive it is or to what extent it implicitly or explicitly honors the five pursuits.

Review Curriculum

When I review curriculum, I research its publishing company and its record for centering equity, justice, and anti-racism. I look at who's on staff (and not on staff) and learn all I can about the backgrounds of the content writers. This information should not be hidden in the curriculum's packaging. Then I read its units for language, looking for key words connected to academics (skills and intellect), cultural competence (identity), sociopolitical consciousness (criticality), and joy. I ask questions such as:

- Do the authors use enough clear language so that teachers at any point in their career can follow the instruction?
- Do the authors use bold and honest language in materials, such as "anti-racism, anti-oppression, and excellence of people of color"?
- Is the instruction written in a way that allows children to come to their own understandings of critical issues or topics?
- Is there guidance for developing skills and intellect only, or is there guidance for developing identity, criticality, and joy, too?

From there, I take responses to the question I asked in Chapter 2, "What child do you hope your instruction and leadership will cultivate?" and compare those responses to what the curriculum offers. For example, if we return to the responses I offered in that chapter, we can look for evidence of those qualities in the curriculum.

1. Empathic
2. Happy and joyful
3. Has knowledge about history and current events
4. Has positive mental health and social-emotional intelligence
5. Inquisitive
6. Kind
7. Loves self and others
8. Problem-solver
9. Skillful across disciplines and contents
10. Socially just and conscious when it comes to race, culture, gender, class, ability, and other intersectional identities

How does the curriculum explicitly teach and access empathy, kindness, and problem-solving? What texts are used to support instruction? I also ask, *Are there moments in the curriculum that recognize and allow students to develop any of the characteristics on this list?* In other words, once I'm familiar with the curriculum's content, if necessary, can I add learning goals, discussion questions, and assessments on empathy, kindness, and problem-solving?

Again, we create these beautiful lists of qualities within our children, but too often curriculum does not promote them or provide ways to develop them in children.

Evaluate Curriculum

I typically use two tools to evaluate curriculum, adapting them as necessary: The CRE Scorecard and the HILL Evaluation. It is best to evaluate a curriculum at a full scale and not in parts. Just one unit, for example, will likely not allow you to find all aspects of the categories of CRE or CHRE.

THE CRE SCORECARD

The CRE Scorecard was developed by the Education Justice Research and Organizing Collaborative (EJ-ROC) at New York University's Metro Center (Bryan-Gooden, Hester & Peoples, 2019). It addresses the importance of identity (e.g., race, class, gender, sexuality, class, ability, and religion), equity, and justice in curriculum and instruction. Due to the historical exclusion people of color and other marginalized groups in books and curriculum, the scorecard is organized into these categories for analysis:

- Representation
- Social Justice
- Teacher Materials

Researchers at the EJ-ROC reported the following, based on their analysis of 15 commonly used English language arts curricula and books for PreK through eighth grade: "White authors and characters are wildly over-represented in proportion to the student population. Of the 1,205 books we analyzed, 1,003 books were by white authors, yet white students represent only 15 percent of NYC's student population. This is nearly five times more books than by all authors of color combined" (Bryan-Gooden, Hester, & Peoples, 2019). In my own reviews, my findings are similar. Most schools still adopt curricula and books for English language arts by white authors, even when their population is 85 percent+ students of color.

Representation: The first part of the CRE Scorecard covers issues of representation in the curriculum, helping evaluators determine the extent to which students are reflected and are being taught about diverse authors, characters, identities, and cultures. The authors of the scorecard assert that evaluators should not confuse representation and tokenism. Educators may think they have a culturally responsive curriculum simply because characters of color are represented in the materials. The first part of the scorecard allows evaluators to determine whether the curriculum truly represents humans for their diversity as well as the accuracy of cultures.

Social Justice: The second part of the scorecard is about social justice, and is divided into three categories, each of which helps the evaluator to understand the opportunities the curriculum provides for cultural responsiveness:

1) Decolonization, Power, and Privilege; 2) Centering Multiple Perspectives; and 3) Connect Learning to Real Life and Action.

Teacher Materials: The third part of the CRE Scorecard focuses on teacher materials. Many districts provide training on how to adapt curriculum to be more culturally and historically responsive, but they don't provide materials that show teachers how to approach areas of CRE ethically and positively. A quality curriculum provides teachers with guidance on how to approach, enhance, and customize lessons to meet the needs of their students. The CRE Scorecard is a powerful tool that can also be adapted and used as a rubric or evaluation.

THE HILL EVALUATION

After studying the five pursuits of the Hill Model, you can review the full curriculum, using the HILL Evaluation on pages 158–160. The curriculum should provide teaching strategies, discussions, reflections, and assessments for each pursuit. If you are reviewing only one unit, it would be key that the final score is above zero and not in the negative range (see scoring guidelines below). Note that each of the pursuits is represented in the evaluation. In this way, you can see the totality of how and to what extent the curriculum represents the HILL Model.

After you've calculated scores for *each* pursuit, examine them to determine the extent of CHRE in that area:

- **+6 to +10: Cultural and Historical Responsiveness is Very Satisfactory**
  Cultural responsiveness is evident in the identified area throughout the entire curriculum.

- **+1 to +5: Cultural and Historical Responsiveness is Satisfactory**
  Cultural responsiveness is evident in the identified area in some parts of the curriculum.

- **-5 to 0: Cultural and Historical Responsiveness is Unclear and Needs Improvement**
  Cultural responsiveness is evident in the identified area in few parts of the curriculum. The area is unclear in the curriculum and is lacking in this area.

- **-10 to -6: There is Little to No Cultural and Historical Responsiveness**
  Cultural responsiveness is not evident in the identified area in any part of the curriculum. The area is almost not seen in the curriculum, or it is very unclear and ambiguous on how youth will have opportunities to advance in this area of CHRE.

The HILL Evaluation

IDENTITY

	+2 Very Satisfactory	+1 Satisfactory	-1 Unclear	-2 Not Satisfactory
1. The curriculum provides opportunities for students to learn or explore their own (cultural) identities in positive ways.				
2. The curriculum provides opportunities for students to learn about the (cultural) identities of others (perhaps different from them).				
3. The curriculum provides diverse identities for learning across the units, and not just solely one identity of a child or others.				
4. The genius and joy of people of color's identities are expressed explicitly.				
5. The curriculum presents the identities of students or others in non-deficit ways.				
Total:				

Curriculum Examples and Suggestions for Revisions:

SKILLS

	+2 Very Satisfactory	+1 Satisfactory	-1 Unclear	-2 Not Satisfactory
1. The curriculum provides opportunities for students to learn a diversity of content-area skills.				
2. The curriculum teaches content-area skills through the exploration of layered multimodal texts.				
3. The curriculum teaches a wide range of literacy skills (opportunities to advance reading, writing, speaking, and thinking).				
4. The curriculum has direction for differentiating, adapting, and advancing the skills through strategies and methods.				
5. The curriculum has skills that allow students to engage in accelerated learning.				
Total:				

Curriculum Examples and Suggestions for Revisions:

INTELLECT

	+2 Very Satisfactory	+1 Satisfactory	-1 Unclear	-2 Not Satisfactory
1. The curriculum provides opportunities for students to become smarter about something (people, places, things, histories, concepts).				
2. The new knowledge taught in the curriculum is clear and explicit.				
3. The curriculum advances students' mental powers and critical thinking.				
4. The curriculum provides diverse topics for intellectualism across the units.				
5. The curriculum provides opportunities for students to put knowledge into action in their schools, communities, or society.				
Total:				

Curriculum Examples and Suggestions for Revisions:

CRITICALITY

	+2 Very Satisfactory	+1 Satisfactory	-1 Unclear	-2 Not Satisfactory
1. The curriculum provides opportunities for students to make sense of/understand systematic power, authority, equity, and/or anti-oppression.				
2. The curriculum advances students' abilities to combat or agitate racism, sexism, classism, or other oppressions related to humanity, lands, environments, or animals.				
3. The curriculum provides diverse criticality topics across the units.				
4. The curriculum provides historically accurate texts and authorship on criticality topics.				
5. The curriculum provides opportunities for students to understand multiple perspectives and the perspectives of historically excluded people.				
Total:				

Curriculum Examples and Suggestions for Revisions:

JOY				
	+2 Very Satisfactory	**+1** Satisfactory	**-1** Unclear	**-2** Not Satisfactory
1. The curriculum elevates beauty in humanity.				
2. The curriculum has opportunities for students to experience poetry, music, and other forms of art.				
3. The curriculum has opportunities for students to experience play, imagination, wonder, and freedom.				
4. The curriculum centers the joy and happiness of historically excluded people.				
5. The curriculum is free of misconceptions of marginalized groups of people and centers truth and genius.				
Total:				
Curriculum Examples and Suggestions for Revisions:				

The Hill Evaluation can be used as a "checklist" for informal review and discussion. If a team is reviewing the curriculum, members should meet to talk about the tool and their informal read of the curriculum. Then each member should rank/score the curriculum individually then return to the team to discuss scores, asking questions such as, *What did we find within each pursuit? What are examples and evidence of our findings? Where were we unsure? Where do we have consensus and disagreement? Does this evaluation provide an accurate picture of the curriculum? Why or why not? Does additional information need to be collected? How do findings of the HILL Evaluation compare to findings of the CRE Scorecard?* After discussion, team members should average out their scores for the total and suggest any modifications to the curriculum materials and text selections.

The findings of the CRE Scorecard's *representation* section should, ideally, align with the findings of the HILL Evaluation's *identity* section. Similarly, the findings of CRE Scorecard's *social justice* section should align greatly with the findings of the Hill Evaluation's *criticality* section.

Once you've gathered and analyzed all qualitative and quantitative data, write a summative statement and report to share with community members, school board members, teachers, and students. If the curriculum is lacking in cultural and historical responsiveness, decisions and policies must shift so students receive the highest quality of instruction.

These two tools can also be used by curriculum publishers for developing protocols and rubrics. Publishing companies should also provide their evaluation results of cultural and historical responsiveness, along with information on who conducted the evaluation. If companies' own employees are evaluating the curriculum, it interrupts the validity of the data.

4. Develop a Protocol for Curriculum Publishers

You could also use the HILL Model to develop a protocol for publishing companies that are providing curriculum to your school or district for adoption consideration. Many cities and towns have rich and beautiful histories related to abolition, yet they are nowhere to be found in the school's curriculum—not even in the social studies curriculum. For example, Black literary societies have a documented history in major cities such as New York, Boston, and Philadelphia, yet unless teachers include that history in the curriculum on their own, it is not typically represented. Content writers at publishing companies ignore it. We must make sure companies are creating something special for each school district. Many companies write curriculum holistically for certain cities or states and not particular districts. Then they merely adapt the curriculum they created, using the district's state standards. To evaluate curriculum, here are questions to ask representatives of publishing company if you serve on adoption committees:

- **Identity:** *What do you know about the identities of the communities we serve in our district? What research have you done on and what have you read about our community? Can you give examples of genius, joy, and beauty in our community that contribute to its identities? We have a population of students of color. How will we see the beauty and essence of their lives manifested across the curriculum? How can you assure us that the curriculum contains truthful narratives and representations of diverse people of the world? How will teacher materials honor students' identities and help teachers to navigate a beautiful understanding of who they teach?*

- **Skills:** *What standards of our state are covered in the curriculum? What if the skills are not accelerated or challenging enough? How will you adapt them? What research-based strategies does it include for the teaching of skills?*

Are they centered on Eurocentric scholarship, or do they embrace critical theories? What theories were considered as the curriculum was being developed? How will teacher materials help teachers to navigate skills and standards through differentiation, accommodations, and strategies?

- **Intellect:** *How does each unit connect to an intellectual topic of the world? What diverse topics and themes are covered? From whose perspectives will those topics and themes be taught? What local histories and topics are addressed in the curriculum? How will teacher materials help to teach new knowledge to students?*

- **Criticality**: *How will the curriculum address topics related to criticality? What topics across the entire curriculum are covered? What topics are not covered, and why? From whose perspectives are those topics being taught? How do the instructional and teacher's materials address issues of equity, bias, anti-racism, anti-oppression, justice, and humanity?*

- **Joy:** *How will the curriculum address joy for students and across humanity? What examples of joy will be written across the curriculum? How does the curriculum incorporate (explicitly) love of self and humanity; caring for and helping humanity and earth; recognizing truth, beauty, aesthetics, art, and wonder; and working to solve social problems of the world?*

Add to these questions as you identify unique needs of your school or district. Once you receive responses, meet with committee members to discuss the wisdom (or lack thereof) in adopting the curriculum and planning needs if you move forward with it.

5. Rely on Read-Alouds and Discussion Questions

Read-alouds of picture books can and should be carried out at any grade level, with children of any age, not just younger children. You can use read-alouds to introduce a complex topic and capture students' attention about it. Start by selecting a text to read aloud, study the author and content, and then determine ways connect the text to student learning and joy. During your reading, pause to look at the illustrations and talk about content with students. After your reading, ask follow-up questions, such as the ones that follow for picture books by Derrick Barnes and Nikole Hannah-Jones and Renée Watson.

The King of Kindergarten or *The Queen of Kindergarten* by Derrick Barnes (Grade K)

> **Identity:** How are you the king or queen of kindergarten?
>
> **Skills:** Can you retell the story and name the events in order? (You can also ask implicit and explicit comprehension questions.)
>
> **Intellect:** What does it mean to be the kings and queens of kindergarten? What are the experiences and responsibilities of kings and queens of kindergarten?
>
> **Criticality:** Why should we recite our names with pride? Why are our names important? How can kings and queens help others who may be sad or discouraged?
>
> **Joy:** What does your "brilliant, beaming, majestic smile" look like? When you look in the mirror, what beauty do you see?

The 1619 Project: Born on the Water by Nikole Hannah-Jones and Renée Watson (Grade 3)

> **Identity:** What did you learn about African people?
>
> **Skills:** What do these vocabulary words mean: *enslaved*, *freedom*, *plateau*, *joy*, and *determination*?
>
> **Intellect:** In what year were Africans captured and forced to the United States? What are some examples of harmful acts in the book?
>
> **Criticality:** What is oppression? How was it shown in the story?
>
> **Joy:** How did African people express happiness, self-love, and joy?

6. Elevate Foundational Skills and Reading Science

Educators often ask how the HILL Model aligns with reading science research. What needs to be understood is that the HILL Model does not interrupt the teaching and learning of foundational reading skills such as letter-name recognition, letter-sound recognition, phonemic awareness, decoding, fluency, vocabulary, and/or comprehension. The model only complements and elevates traditional reading skills. However, many traditional reading programs don't take into consideration students' lives and the world around them. Adding the framework to a traditional lesson or unit plan will lift student learning and help them to retain the skills and strategies. Earlier in the book, I offered a unit plan for decoding based on the framework. You will observe a big difference when you teach skills and strategies in contextualized ways. It's important to connect learning to students' lives and the world around them, every chance you get.

On a related note, you can approach small-group reading instruction differently by asking comprehension questions related to culturally and historically responsive teaching and learning. For example, for this book, *I See Bugs* by Wiley Blevins, I do just that:

Identity: What bugs have you seen or learned about? What do you think of bugs?

Skills: Students will learn how to read with accuracy.

Intellect: What is something you learned about bugs?

Criticality: Should bugs be protected? Why? How do certain bugs help to keep up the world?

Joy: What is your favorite bug, and why? Can you name different bugs and their colors?

In reading groups, the selected text becomes more meaningful—and can strengthen reading development—when discussion questions are based on CHRE pursuits. It can also increase students' interest and motivation to read about, engage in, and study new topics. You can incorporate an element of play as students rotate across reading groups and learning centers, as a way for students to comprehend texts and learn about the world around them. Consider creating play centers for PreK to draw bugs, count bugs, dig for bugs, be a bug, or decode bug words.

Lastly, for the upper grades, the HILL Model can be used as an annotation strategy, where students read literary fiction or nonfiction and use the five pursuits as a framework for analyzing the text and writing notes. Here is the opening paragraph to the popular short story *Thank You, M'am* by Langston Hughes.

> She was a large woman with a large purse that had everything in it but hammer and nails. It had a long strap, and she carried it slung across her shoulder. It was about eleven o'clock at night, and she was walking alone, when a boy ran up behind her and tried to snatch her purse. The strap broke with the single tug the boy gave it from behind. But the boy's weight and the weight of the purse combined caused him to lose his balance so, instead of taking off full blast as he had hoped, the boy fell on his back on the sidewalk, and his legs flew up. The large woman simply turned around and kicked him right square in his blue-jeaned sitter. Then she reached down, picked the boy up by his shirt front, and shook him until his teeth rattled.

After reading the passage, students can increase reading comprehension by using the following questions as a guide to annotate the text.

Identity: What did I learn about the identity(ies) of the character? What language speaks to identity?

Skills: How does the author use language to build momentum? How does the author use punctuation in interesting ways? Show evidence of this. Predict what will happen next and add to your annotations.

Intellect: What new knowledge did I gain from the passage?

Criticality: What is the problem in the text?

Joy: What examples of beauty of language are presented in the passage?

After reading the passage (or the entire story), students can individually or collaboratively annotate it by connecting their understanding to the five pursuits. Of course, this strategy should first be modeled by the teacher. This is a way to engage with text in an unconventional way, while strengthening reading comprehension. If writing development is your priority, students can read the text like a writer.

7. Try Lesson Plans if Time Is Tight

A lesson plan is typically carried out in a single school week, so it is more abbreviated than a unit plan. If your time is tight, use a lesson plan to incorporate the HILL Model. In the following example, I chose a topic I wanted to learn about and teach: the history of the Chicano Youth Movement. While this is a wide and comprehensive topic, I found ways to abbreviate it by applying the pursuits, which allowed me to carry out instruction and assessment within the week. For this lesson plan, I engaged students in a study about the beauty and genius of Chicano people. I learned from scholars and activists in the community and read many multimodal texts to prepare. Then I addressed the five pursuits this way:

Two Chicano youth at the 1970 march in Los Angeles

Identity: Students will learn about Chicano culture. (*Assessment: student discussion*)

Students will identify what they would like to change and keep in their own schools. (*Assessment: student-written lists*)

Skills: Students will cite textual evidence from informational text. (*Assessment: ELA quiz*)

Intellect: Students will learn about Chicano student protests in California. (*Assessment: ELA quiz*)

Criticality: Students will identify issues related to schools today and how they affect the education of children. They will learn how young people have a voice for social and educational change. (*Assessment: collaborative discussion*)

Joy: Students will examine how improved schools and education create more safe and engaging spaces for youth. They will examine Chicano resistance art. (*Assessment: collaborative art compositions*)

This lesson can be layered with texts such as videos, images of youth protest, and primary source documents such as newspaper articles, youth poetry, and lists of demands for education written by children.

8. Create Unit Plans for Deep Learning

Unit plans, which are designed to be taught in more than one week, are the most typical way the HILL Model is implemented in classrooms. Unit plans generally take between three to six weeks to carry out. The exact timeframe should be based on a number of criteria: the pursuits and standards you want to address, the amount of reading students need to do, the learning experiences students will engage in, and your assessment of student learning. Of course, you can explore the pursuits more deeply, regardless of which ones you choose, because a unit plan allows more time.

When planning a unit, consider pacing, materials, students' prior knowledge and skills, and what students need personally and academically. Below are some examples of unit plans related to the natural elements of the earth that span content areas and grade levels. These unit pursuits can be expanded into full unit plans where the various parts of the unit are added. (See the Legacy Plan Template in Chapter 4.) Within each unit, I try to make family/caregiver connections so that the learning that's happening in the classroom is amplified at home and a partnership forms. Please be mindful of students who do not live in traditional homes and may be experiencing housing insecurity.

Natural Elements of the Earth

ELEMENTARY SCHOOL (AIR)

Identity: I can study the air quality in my local community, town, or city.

Skills:

- **Art:** I can study textures artists use to depict air and the sky or to respond to environmental justice.
- **English Language Arts:** I can ask and answer questions about key details in a text.
- **Physical Education/Health/Wellness:** I can learn how to measure my heart rate when moving, walking, or running.
- **Social Studies:** I can learn about the history of air pollution.
- **Math:** I can learn that the numbers from 11 to 19 are composed of a ten and one, two, three, four, five, six, seven, eight, or nine ones (Grade 1: numerical thinking about animals and items in sky/air).
- **Science:** I can communicate solutions that will reduce the impact of humans on the land, water, air, and/or other living things in the local environment.

Intellect: I can learn about the importance of air quality.

Criticality: I can learn about pollution that disproportionately harms underserved communities.

Joy: I can learn about the beautiful things the sky and air contain, such as birds, clouds, and rainbows.

- **Family/Home Connection:** Document the daily air quality index in your community, town, or city, and make observations of what you observe in the air.

MIDDLE AND HIGH SCHOOL (WATER)

Identity: I can identify the significance of water in our daily lives.

Skills:

- **Art:** I can study watercolor and its visual effects.
- **English Language Arts:** I can distinguish among fact, opinion, and reasoned judgment in a text.
- **Physical Education/Health/Wellness:** I can learn why it's important to drink water while exercising.
- **Social Studies:** I can determine the central ideas or key information in a secondary source, and provide an accurate summary of the source that isn't based on my prior knowledge or opinions.
- **Math:** I can learn units of measurement, including the volume of a liquid.
- **Science:** I can understand how water is purified.

Intellect: I can learn about places in the world where clean water is widely available—and places it isn't.

Criticality: I can understand the global importance of access to clean water and how water quality is an environmental justice issue.

Joy: I can learn how water is healing and healthy for humanity.

- **Family/Home Connection:** Make a list of ways we can conserve water to ensure a healthier planet for all.

ADULT EDUCATION (RESPONSIBILITIES OF THE EARTH)

Identity: Students will consider their choices, roles, and responsibilities regarding the earth to determine the impact they have.

Skills:

- **Art:** Students will study a visual work of art depicting humans' responsibilities to the earth.
- **English Language Arts and Science:** Students will conduct a short research project investigating an environmental issue and proposing solutions to it, presenting claims, findings, relevant evidence, and valid reasoning.
- **Physical Education/Health/Wellness:** Students will identify how taking care of the earth leads to human wellness and health.
- **Social Studies:** Students will understand how human activities help shape the earth's surface.
- **Math:** Students will calculate and interpret the average rate of change of a function over a specified interval.

Intellect: Students will research one environmental problem and define it, the history of it, and the current state of it.

Criticality: Students will identify environmental problems our planet faces to determine solutions.

Joy: Students will name examples of the growth and progress of nature when humans make decisions that help the environment.

HIGHER EDUCATION (LEGACY TO THE EARTH)

Identity: Preservice teachers/teacher candidates will consider the legacy they want to leave on the earth. When it comes to teaching, what legacy(ies) do you want to leave on the earth?

Skills: Preservice teachers/teacher candidates will consider ways to increase and sustain professional knowledge and pedagogical skills. How will you water the earth?

Intellect: Preservice teachers/teacher candidates will learn about five new critical theorists (waterers) of education and the implications of their theories for the classroom.

Criticality: Preservice teachers/teacher candidates will learn about historical and systemic racism, oppressive problems of the educational systems, and why we need to unearth solutions.

Joy: Preservice teachers/teacher candidates will learn the beauty of the profession and how to claim joy, wellness, and self-care in the field. They will create a metaphor related to the earth that represents their teaching.

- **Family/Home Connection:** Who supports you in your village as you strive to offer children the best education possible?

Post-Instruction

9. Ask Students End-of-Unit Questions

Many teachers have told me that it can be difficult to incorporate the five pursuits into every unit they plan, largely because of time constraints. In response, I tell them to start with one unit at a time, which can be a more comfortable way to gradually develop expertise. For teachers who don't use the HILL Model, the next example could help pave the way. The teacher carries out traditional unit plans and uses the days after the unit to create space for students to come to their own CHRE understandings of the five pursuits. Those days should be spent discussing, reflecting, and writing to respond to student learning. For example, here are questions that would enable students to come to their own inquiry-based understanding from a math unit:

Identity: How did the *mathematical* learning help you to learn about yourself and your mathematical identity?

Skills: How did the *mathematical* learning build upon your current math skills? Where do you still struggle?

Intellect: How did the *mathematical* learning connect to the world?

Criticality: How did the *mathematical* learning relate to problems in the world?

Joy: How did the *mathematical* learning connect to beauty, problem-solving, or joy? How did it make you feel when you experienced success and independence?

Of course, this is a math example, but you can adapt it so that it connects to any of the content areas you teach. If time permits, you can extend your reflections and have students create projects or administer a culminating assessment based on their *criticality* responses to the problems of the world. From there, students can go deeper by working together on a project to solve one of those problem, using math skills, among other skills.

10. Assume the Role of Action Researcher

Finally, the HILL Model can be used as a post-unit assessment. You assume the role of action researcher to collect formal or informal data on student learning by asking questions of individual students, small groups of students, or the whole class. The questions can be asked in a variety of formats: as casual conversation, more structured discussion, interviews, or as surveys to save time. If you have a paraprofessional, a partner in education, ask them to help you collect information on how students experienced the five pursuits during the unit.

1. What do you think about what you learned in this unit?
2. How do you think your classmates would respond to what they learned? How does your own experience compare?
3. If you could add a different text to read during our learning, what would it be?
4. What did you learn about yourself or others? How did it feel to learn about identity?
5. What new skills did you learn and get an opportunity to practice? How do you feel about your ability to practice those skills independently?
6. What new knowledge did you gain? Is that knowledge useful to your life?
7. What did you learn about justice? How will that criticality-related topic help you in life?
8. Did you learn about joy? How important is joy to you?
9. What did you like best about the unit and what you learned from it?
10. What would you change to elevate the unit?

These questions can be adapted depending on your students' ages and levels of understanding. What's most important is that we get rich feedback from those we serve and to whom we are most accountable: our students.

What Flowers Will You Paint?

"I paint flowers so they will not die."

—FRIDA KAHLO

There is no one way to paint. There is no one way to create. There is certainly no one way to use the HILL Model to help students learn and grow. I hope you see its instructional versatility and take something beautiful and add layers of beauty to the model. If teaching and learning are artistic processes, *what should we paint?* By reading the strategies and examples I've provided in this chapter, I hope I've brought you closer to understanding the model and each of the five pursuits. Please know, as long as you stay true to the essence and purpose of the model, those strategies and examples can be adapted, modified as you see fit to meet the needs of your students and their learning. And always keep in mind, the model can be extended across grades PreK–12, adult education, higher education, and other educational spaces.

Chapter 5 Reflection

Select one or more questions to engage in a freewrite.

- **What are some reactions and reflections you have about the music, art, and text from Chapter 5?**
- **What ideas and passages stand out for you and why?**
- **What parts do you want to explore and learn about more?**
- **What parts of the educational system have helped you to grow?**
- **Which parts of the educational system are in need of water?**
- **What do you plan to do to unearth genius and joy?**

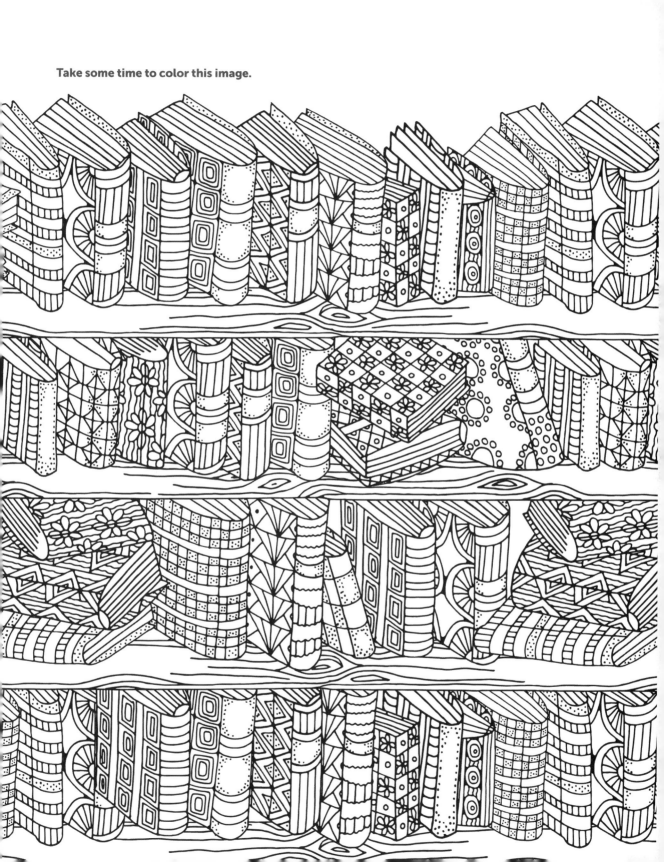

CHAPTER 6

Practical and Creative Uses of the HILL Model:

School Leaders, Community Members, and Families

LAYERED PLAYLIST

Songs that inspire me about strong leadership and support. Play them as you read this chapter.

"O-o-h Child,"
The Five Stairsteps

"Talkin' 'bout a Revolution,"
Tracy Chapman

"The Revolution Will Not Be Televised,"
Gil Scott-Heron

"Imagine," John Lennon

"Beautiful Day," U2

"Flowers," Kelly Rowland

"Redemption Song,"
Bob Marley & the Wailers

"I Dream a World,"
Elements of Life

"Wildflowers,"
Tom Petty

"Follow Me," Aly-Us

"We are each other's harvest; we are each other's business; we are each other's magnitude and bond."

—GWENDOLYN BROOKS

Our Land
by Langston Hughes

We should have a land of sun,
Of gorgeous sun,
And a land of fragrant water
Where the twilight
Is a soft bandanna handkerchief
Of rose and gold,
And not this land where life is cold.

We should have a land of trees,
Of tall thick trees
Bowed down with chattering parrots
Brilliant as the day,
And not this land where birds are grey.

Ah, we should have a land of joy,
Of love and joy and wine and song,
And not this land where joy is wrong.

Oh, sweet away!
Ah, my beloved one, away!

Unearthing Thought

1. How do you define leadership?

2. What are roles and responsibilities of leaders?

3. What are your special interests in and talents for leadership?

4. Is culturally and historically responsive education possible without strong leaders at the center? If not, why is leadership key for successful implementation?

5. Where do you notice the five pursuits in policies, equity plans, equity documents, recruitment and interview protocols, mission statements, and other leadership tools?

6. When designing (or helping to design) policies and protocols, what feelings and emotions do you experience?

7. In what ways could the five pursuits be enacted at a leadership level?

8. What role should district and school leaders play when it comes to implementing culturally and historically responsive teaching and learning

9. What systemic and instructional changes are needed in your school, district, or university, given the current landscape?

10. What barriers do leaders face when adopting and overseeing culturally and historically responsive programs? What are constructive responses to those barriers?

CHRE Leadership Matters for the Harvest

The harvest of genius and joy would not happen without the dedication and strength of excellent leaders. We are all leading on Indigenous lands, creating landscapes and environments that advance the five pursuits for all visitors and all those who have a stake in education, which arguably should be every human. Ultimately, as Langston Hughes poetically put it, "We should have a land of joy." CHRE will not be fully realized in any educational space unless it is embraced and embodied by its leaders. Leaders are essential to ensuring the foundational culture and environment that's necessary for implementing CHRE. Without them, some educators will likely apply CHRE in their practices, whereas others will not. Without policy, we will not observe CHRE throughout a school system. Some teachers know that they have been hired without the expectation of CHRE and have maintained their positions. Therefore, they may resist CHRE practices, even when students need it. I ask, *Why is this?* Whenever school unions, organizations, boards, and administrators don't move from verbal expectations to written polices, they create space for mediocrity, culturally and historically *unresponsive* work, or oppressive practices. This has been taking place in education for decades.

This chapter takes on issues of leadership, while offering potential solutions by showing how the HILL Model and the five pursuits can help create a culture for all communities we serve. When I use the word "leader," I am referring to anyone who has been (self)appointed, hired, or expected to elevate an educational environment and those within it, including teacher leaders, academic coaches, content specialists, school board members, parent coordinators, non-direct instructional staff, superintendents, district-level administrators, principals, assistant principals, teacher educators, and anyone else who has leadership gifts and knowledge. CHRE and efforts to increase equity must not be the sole "job" or "responsibility" of the Black teachers or a special committee. I find that whenever racism comes up at staff meetings, some can look to people of color, particularly Black folks, to be the "voice"—the ones to respond. Often, when racism is raised, we, people of color, are grieving and feeling deep pain. We see brothers and sisters killed daily, and it is difficult to even wake up in the morning, let alone be a voice of reason, explanation, or solutions. Equity, anti-racism, and CHRE must be the work of us all, not just of those who are most affected by it. I try to keep in mind that most teachers are hired to educate children and not their colleagues, but sometimes they do take on leadership roles. Yet it's important for them to be mindful of their own wellness, energy, and capacity to have multiple roles and responsibilities.

It is easy to be ignorant. It takes work to maintain genius.

The professional knowledge—the genius—of leaders must be a priority. The cultivation of genius as expressed in this book happens in a variety of ways. To lead, one must first read scholarship and the world. Leaders must seek the knowledge—historical and current—related to the field of education. It is easy to be ignorant. It takes work to maintain genius. We tell young people to resist swimming in a pool of ignorance and, instead, to go into the world being lifelong learners, but then I see leaders who haven't read anything beyond their old white male theorists in college. Admittedly, it is difficult to find time to grow professionally, given the demands of work and family. So I suggest starting by going on a "cultivating genius diet" of knowledge building by reading, watching, or listening to a short text each week.

Leaders must also involve themselves in professional development. I encourage them to be present at all trainings centered on equity and CHRE. In all my years of witnessing such trainings from grant and research work, including in a district that hosted over 30 sessions, not one principal, superintendent, administrator, or district leader showed up to learn alongside or support teachers. The teachers have typically gone back to their classrooms to apply the HILL Model, with their principals having no knowledge of it and, therefore, no ways to support them. This is like having a basketball coach with no knowledge of how to play the game. The model cannot be implemented effectively if teachers are working alone. Administrators must understand it and, ideally, participate in the teaching and learning that's happening in classrooms. Of course, the absence of leaders has made teachers feel their administrators are not serious about this work and will not know what to look for when they visit classrooms.

Too often, leaders offer trainings and sessions so they can "check off" CHRE and others can see they "did the work." But that is clearly not the work. It is only presenting on paper that something CHRE-related is being done. Rather, leaders must be forthright about CHRE and lead through words and actions. They must sustain the work over time. They must also teach. Even if it is just one period a year, every teacher leader, academic coach, content specialist, school board member, superintendent, district-level administrator, principal, assistant principal, and other leaders must teach a CHRE learning experience if they are going to lead CHRE efforts. They must be excellent pedagogues to lead schools and districts effectively. They must commit to CHRE by creating a plan for schools and districts, detailing why this work matters and including actionable steps that will ensure it is implemented smoothly and strategically. CHRE must be a part of every speech, report, and strategic plan. The leaders who are most successful at implementing the HILL Model:

- Cultivate excellent mentors and critical educators in their village.
- Follow research in education and of instructional and leadership methods.

- Gain knowledge of multiple educational theories, including critical theories.
- Keep up with and read leadership-related texts.
- Understand how to write curriculum and teach in excellent ways.
- Seize professional learning opportunities that relate to equity, justice, anti-racism, and CHRE, and actively partner with their teachers and follow up with actions.
- Tell the truth boldly and unapologetically.
- Collect data on identity, intellect, criticality, and joy, as well as skills, truancy, test scores, and school climate.
- Know how to write position statements and policy, using prudent and educative language.

This is just a short list. I find that the strongest leaders are strong scholars and "doers" of the word and content of CHRE. They know how to do what they ask and expect of their teachers and staff. And if they don't know how, they partner with those who can teach them.

10 Creative Ways to Use the HILL Model

As I said in Chapter 5, the HILL Model can be mandated, adopted, suggested, and encouraged across any school or district. If "mandating" feels too stringent, consider why. We have witnessed states push, pass, and, indeed, mandate anti-Black policies and very hurtful guidelines. But they never mandate CHRE. For example, look at your school or district handbook for language related to CHRE policy and practices. Is it there? And if it is, is it clear? Our CHRE definitions and guides must be aligned with policies of teacher unions, teacher and leader evaluation, and mandated standards and curriculum.

Unfortunately, there are parents and community members who have the time and energy (what a privilege that must be) to travel to school districts, advocating for anti-Black policies and anti-CRE/CHRE practices. If we do not make CHRE documented policy, we will see a constant push against it year after year, and it will become increasingly difficult to sustain. That is precisely why educators say, "We are doing that equity work again, just like 10 years ago." Yes, we are. We never stop because we've never made it policy.

To that end, here are ten ways the model has been used by leaders. Extend or modify the supporting examples to meet the needs of your school or district.

1. Create a Board Policy for Culturally and Historically Responsive Education

Like many readers, I keep a close eye on educational policy and legislation that states and districts push, and those they ignore. I ask: *Have the people who have written this policy or legislation ever written a CHRE lesson or unit plan? Have they loved or taught children of color?* Moreover, board members are typically appointed or elected without having any knowledge of how to write or teach curriculum—and curriculum is the foundation of learning in schools. Having served as a school board member and president, I understand the great responsibility school boards carry. I also know how naturally the work came to me because I came from the field of education. Yet many board members do not have a background in educational policy, leadership, educational research or curriculum and instruction. Consider (if possible) how we recruit and sustain our CHRE board members. Consider what they should know and do before they begin their appointment. Here are some questions to spur your thinking.

- What types of community and cultural knowledge must CHRE board members have and be able to share prior to their start date?
- How do we design or redesign their pre-training and help them to be effective CHRE board members? We might create book clubs, literary societies, mentoring programs, and professional learning sessions centered on the content of the HILL Model and critical scholarship.
- What types of professional learning or development do CHRE board members need to maintain their understanding of equity and anti-racism?
- How many times per school year should CHRE board members engage in teaching and learning with students in the district?
- How can CHRE board members build relationships with teachers, parents, and community members?
- How serious are CHRE board members about creating and approving a CHRE board policy?

On pages 181 and 182, you'll find a draft of a sample policy that CHRE board members can use as a starting point for moving this work forward. A CHRE policy must contain language on equity and anti-racism. I have seen districts around the United States adopt such language and begin to work toward living the statements they approve.

When revising this draft for your own purposes, be sure to take into consideration previous written policies around equity and anti-racism that your district has approved and implemented.

Culturally and Historically Responsive Education Policy

Adopted Date: _____

The _____ Board of Education adheres to and adopts a model of Culturally and Historically Responsive Education (CHRE) across PreK–12 schools and rejects any form of discrimination, racism, and other forms of oppression, as this is in violation of the School District's values, goals, beliefs, vision, and mission. CHRE is a model and framework of education that honors multiple and effective theories of education, including cognitive, sociocultural, and critical theories of teaching, learning, and leadership.

Purpose of CHRE Policy

The purpose of this policy is to establish an understanding and create a set of protocols and practices toward CHRE within school climate, leadership, curriculum, and instruction. This CHRE Policy honors and extends the Board's previous policies related to equity and anti-racism, condemning any form of hate, violence, white supremacy, or harm inflicted (implicitly or explicitly) upon anyone within the district.

The CHRE Policy requires that educators learn, teach, and lead across five pursuits of education that ensure that every child is given opportunities to improve and advance their growth in the areas of:

1. **Identity:** Ensuring that students learn their histories and racial/other cultural identities while also learning the truth and knowledge about others who are different from their own identities. This also involves teaching students to make sense of their own values, perspectives, and beliefs.

2. **Skills:** Ensuring that students learn the adopted state standards and content-area proficiencies across disciplines and grade levels. Skills are also central in designing the learning standards that govern teaching and learning in schools. Each content area has its own descriptions and set of skills that youth are expected to master and teachers are expected to teach.

3. **Intellect:** Ensuring that students learn new knowledge about various topics and ideas across the global context. Intellect is knowledge into action and involves learning to think deeply and apply skills.

4. **Criticality:** Ensuring that students learn the ability to understand power, oppression, anti-racism, and anti-oppression. Criticality calls for teachers and students to understand the ideologies and perspectives of historically excluded people and communities and their ways of knowing and experiencing the world.

5. **Joy:** Ensuring that students learn and experience happiness and triumphs by elevating beauty and truth in themselves and other people, stories, and histories. Joy involves the teaching and learning of love of self and humanity, solutions to the social problems of the world.

continued

Culturally and Historically Responsive Education Policy continued

It is essential that the five components are taught together and not in isolation and that educators diversify the topics and type of identities, skills and learning standards, intellectual topics, criticality topics, and joy-related learning across the academic year. The Board is committed to supporting each teacher, leader, and staff member by helping to increase knowledge and professional practice. The goal is to create a CHRE Strategic Plan to be implemented that would ensure each educator enacts CHRE so that low achievement is reduced as well as improving a low student personal and sociocultural development. Therefore, this policy is a response to the need to dismantle and disrupt racism, poor or limited goals for education, ineffective pedagogical methods, lack of diversity in content, teaching, text selections, and pedagogical practices, and other economic, social, and educational inequities. It is understood that the five pursuits of CHRE is a departure from the ways education has been structured and mandated since the inception of formal schools; this is why the CHRE Strategic Plan is key for dismantling and rebuilding a system that is centered within more than just skill development and assessment. This policy promotes higher excellence in education and ensures that all educators' and children's histories, identities, literacies, and liberation are reflected and taught in schools. To this end, this CHRE Board Policy must reflect evaluations, observations, trainings, and other means of professional learning.

CHRE Processes and Directives

These processes and directives will be provided within the District. Each document must embody explicit language and meaning of equity, anti-racism and CHRE.

The District shall create or adapt the following documents:

- Annual equity and CHRE audit by outside agency
- Curriculum review and evaluation
- Report on changes/revisions in curriculum and instruction
- Guide on how to select curriculum for District
- Revised leader and teacher evaluation
- Guide for recruiting, hiring, and keeping CHRE educators
- Guide for partnering with university teacher education program and listing courses needed for hiring their graduates
- Districtwide professional learning plan

Each of the District schools and buildings shall create or adapt the following documents to be approved by the Board.

- Mission and vision statement
- Student, parent, faculty, and staff handbooks
- Collecting exemplars of CHRE lessons and unit plans
- Data collection and reporting procedures
- Annual equity and CHRE professional learning and assessment plan
- Supporting programs for BIPOC staff, parents, and students

2. Outline Equity Plans

Equity plans outline the ways a school will embrace and act on CHRE practices. Your plan should open with a mission or vision statement that is grounded in the language of inclusion and criticality, and it should answer questions such as:

- What do we want to be known for at our school?
- What are we setting out to do? What are our goals? How will we know if we've met our goals?
- What does the data tell us and not tell us?

As an action item, leaders can come up with three measurable equity goals for the school, based on one of the above components.

3. Organize Professional Development Workshops or Conferences

I have had the opportunity to organize professional development workshops and conferences centered on the HILL Model. These workshops and conferences are important because, too often, teacher education programs do not fully prepare new teachers for culturally responsive or sociopolitically conscious practice. Therefore, effective school leaders offer professional development to fill in the gaps.

Professional development workshops and conferences should be intellectually grounded by encouraging teachers to read, write, and think deeply. They should provide thinking spaces to improve the heart and the mind. But they should also put strategies and models into teachers' hands. I encourage leaders to think creatively. Rather than the traditional lecture-style PD, sessions could include virtual or live instructional modeling, instructional coaching,

Components to Consider for Your Equity Plan

- Overview of equity and CHRE education and causes of inequities
- Overview of the need for equity and CHRE centered beliefs and practices at our school
- Professional development for leaders
- Professional development for teachers
- Professional development for staff members
- Supports for students
- Recruiting and hiring of diverse leaders, teachers, and staff
- Retention of diverse leaders, teachers, and staff
- Ways to create a safe and inclusive environment
- Committees and programs
- Committee and programs evaluation
- Curriculum and instruction
- Evaluation of curriculum and instruction
- Research-supported practices and programs to advance equity
- Data collection and analysis
- Family and community partnerships and engagements

lesson study, or simply an opportunity for teachers to plan together. Regardless of format, school and district leaders should plan to attend. If they don't, teachers will question whether the work will be supported and sustained.

It then becomes essential to find qualified facilitators, perhaps experienced teachers, or leaders in the district, who can deliver training sessions.

We cannot assume that a university's teacher education program is enough to prepare our teachers and leaders for this work. Also, we must not rely solely on outside consultants and other partners to move teachers and leaders toward culturally and historically responsive instruction. It is our responsibility to prepare our facilitators to lead and train others.

Pursuits for Coaches

However professional learning looks, it is key to use the HILL Model to develop learning goals for trainers and participants. Here is an example of those goals:

Identity: Coaches will learn about their professional identities and personal styles for leading professional development.

Skills: Coaches will learn new methods, strategies, and models of leadership.

Intellect: Coaches will learn new theories of education and topics to teach.

Criticality: Coaches will learn how to center justice, anti-racism, and equity in their leadership.

Joy: Coaches will elevate truths, benefits, and beauty of the profession.

Pursuits for Conference Participants

If you're leading an entire conference, you can use the HILL Model to set holistic goals for participants:

> **Identity:** Conference participants will engage in sessions where they learn about the diverse identities of children they serve.
>
> **Skills:** Conference participants will learn new skills, methods, and strategies of teaching and learning.
>
> **Intellect:** Conference participants will learn new theories of education and topics to teach.
>
> **Criticality:** Conference participants will learn how to center justice, anti-racism, and equity in their teaching and learning.
>
> **Joy:** Conference participants will elevate truths, benefits, and beauty of the profession.

Joy Retreats

Create a space to experience joy, where you can recognize and celebrate teachers, students, parents, and staff members. It should be a safe space that members of your community can visit regularly to heal and develop liberatory wellness. Strive to make retreats creative and engaging by including activities such as meditation, yoga, dancing/movement, and/or slow breathing.

Checklist for Staff Members Who Do Not Provide Direct Instruction

In addition to teachers, you likely have wonderful staff members who are often parents' and community members' first line of contact. They may include front-desk professionals, administrative assistants, and those who maintain the building. As such, we must consider what the five pursuits look like for their professional learning and practice.

> **Identity:** Ensure that staff members learn about the history and beauty of the cultures served in the community, including language, religions, race, and other cultures. This will help them to communicate with, love, and treat community members respectfully.
>
> **Skills:** Ensure that staff members learn positive and enabling communication skills, including critical listening to parents and others.
>
> **Intellect:** Ensure that staff members learn about the history of the community and school culture.
>
> **Criticality:** Ensure that staff members are properly educated on histories and current manifestations of equity, justice, racism, and oppression.
>
> **Joy:** Ensure that staff members know how to make visitors feel at home when they enter the school, feel loved when they're in the building, and feel joy when they leave.

4. Examine Your Mission Statement

Your mission statement should not be just romanticized language that sounds good on paper and is never put into action. I believe every school or district's mission is key because it sets a tone, communicates beliefs, and establishes a purpose for education. It is worth the time to sit and discuss the language of your statement as a community and determine to what extent the five pursuits are embedded. You may plan a workshop where you look at your current mission statement and ask: *Has our statement changed or evolved over time? If so, in what ways?* Team members should ask themselves: *What is brilliant and strong about the statement and what needs reworking?* After that, members should have a deep and honest conversation about how devotedly educators have been carrying out the mission. We want to make sure our statements don't just look and sound good but also convey the ways in which we create culture and make decisions daily. Below are questions I use when I am examining mission statements and having open dialogues with stakeholders:

Identity: How does our school or district's mission statement speak to the importance of teaching, learning, validating, or celebrating identities of our students and others?

Skills and Intellect: How does our school or district's mission statement speak to the importance of academic success?

Criticality: How does our school or district's mission statement speak to the importance of justice, liberation, equity, anti-racism, and other anti-oppressions?

Joy: How does our school or district's mission statement speak to the importance of elevating happiness, truth, and beauty in the world?

Here is a sample mission statement that honors the ideas in this book. Use it as a starting point if you are just beginning to take a fresh look at your mission.

The mission of _____ School is to help students to advance in the areas of personal and academic success. We believe in cultivating the genius and joy inside of each child by promoting identity development, skills and proficiencies, intellectualism, criticality, and joy. To this end, we work in every aspect of the students' learning within and outside of the classroom to give culturally and historically responsive education connected to their lives. It is our goal to help each student honor and celebrate their identities while learning about the truths and histories of others who are different than them. We strive to promote intellectually rigorous standards that help youth achieve academically but also how to navigate a global society.

> Through curriculum and instruction, we believe in embracing diversity and justice for global and multicultural perspectives. This will give our students rich ideas and teach them to be independent yet collaborative while striving for a better humanity for all.

5. Rethink Staff Meetings

Each moment of the day offers an opportunity for a leader to create a culture of justice, inclusion, and equity. Staff meetings provide leaders with a space to engage in supportive practices. Because of COVID-19, there has been a shift at many schools in how staff meetings are opened and run. Lots of leaders, myself included, shifted from typical agendas to agendas that center our hearts, wellness, and joy, and we used art and music to create energy and excitement for collaboration. Here are suggestions for getting the most out of staff meetings.

Open With Freedom Songs

Ask each staff member for a song that inspires teaching and learning, and create a playlist to play at the start and close of each meeting. Sometimes positive music can be motivating and engaging. Of course, other forms of art (e.g., visual art, poetry) could work, too.

Ask Turn-and-Talk Questions

At the start of the meeting, ask teachers questions such as:

- How's your heart?
- What have you done for liberatory wellness?
- How is your joy today?
- What is a moment of inspiration teaching you have had?

You can also open meetings with songs and questions connected to the HILL Model. Here are some examples.

Song: "New Beginning" by Tracy Chapman

> **Identity:** Which cultural practices of our students hold great teachable lessons for us?
>
> **Skills:** What are some skills you use to "make a new beginning" each day to learn new advanced methods for teaching and learning?
>
> **Intellect:** What makes a *new beginning* when you are overwhelmed?

Criticality: How is the world "broken into fragments and pieces," and how can we move toward a "unified whole" in our teaching and learning?

Joy: What "new beginnings" will you practice in your classroom?

Song: "Lovely Day" by Bill Withers

Identity: Who do you look to for inspiration?

Skills: What are some skills you need to (re)claim your day?

Intellect: What makes a *lovely day*?

Criticality: What do you do when, at the end of your day, you feel defeated?

Joy: How many times does Bill Withers say "lovely day" in the song?

Song: "Overjoyed" by Stevie Wonder

Identity: Can you describe a moment when you felt overjoyed at school or during your career in education?

Skills: How do you create spaces of joy for students?

Intellect: How do you define joy?

Criticality: In what areas of the educational system do you see joy being decentered? Where is joy missing from the educational system? Why do you think that's so? How do you respond?

Joy: Think about this line from Stevie Wonder's song: "I had found what I've searched to discover." What have you searched for and discovered about your own joy in the profession? What is beautiful about self-discovery?

Ask Identity Self-Reflection Questions

Ask questions that will enable teachers to unpack their identities, bias, genius, and practices.

Example: *What have you learned about yourself today? Name one situation that related to race, racism, or equity. What happened? How did you respond? What would you do the same or differently if it happened again? What engaging and compelling thing have you read or written? How does this impact your professional work?*

Unearth Genius

Describe and show a visual representation of a person, place, moment, or movement to teachers and ask how the knowledge they gain may help them in their lives. Examples:

- Show an image of Black engineer Raye Montague, the first person to design a Naval ship using a computer, and discuss her genius and contribution to the world.
- Show an image of Black mathematician Gladys Mae West, who was instrumental in developing the Global Positioning System (GPS), and ask educators how they may teach this person, her invention, and/or her history in their content area.

Highlight Current Events

Name and summarize a current event and ask teachers how they might teach it or connect it to their content standards.

Share CHRE Data

Rather than only sharing data related to standardized test scores, share data you and teachers have collected on identity growth or joy. Use any of the assessment questions used in this book as a starting place.

Plan Mini-PD Moments

Ask teachers to sign up for an "each one, teach one" presentation, where they each briefly demonstrate an effective strategy or method.

Share Criticality or Joy Videos

Select a short video, screen it at the meeting, and ask teachers to respond to it. There are lots of videos to choose from that elicit joy/laughter but also critical thought. Know your teachers to determine which one they need most.

Engage in CHRE Lesson Plan Study

Put teachers in small groups, show them a lesson plan, and ask them to react to it or critique it.

6. Interview New Teachers and Staff Members Through a CHRE Lens

If leaders seek equitable and culturally responsive teachers, they must ask them a unique set of questions—questions that relate to what they value in teachers. If equity, anti-oppression, and justice matter, direct questions about those topics must be asked. The authors of a recent Edutopia article on interviewing teachers provided common questions that effective leaders ask (2019). Here are some of them:

- Why did you decide to become a teacher?
- How do you cultivate positive relationships with your students and create a sense of class community?
- Do you incorporate collaborative and project-based learning?
- How do you include parents and guardians in their child's education?
- How do you maintain your own professional development, and what areas would you select for your personal growth?

These are good questions. They certainly could elicit powerful responses. But I ask: *How might you revise any of them to be more grounded in equity?* As these questions stand, they will not help in hiring a sociopolitical-conscious teacher who embraces anti-racist practices. They will not help leaders to understand how the candidate will advance and accelerate the learning of culturally, racially, and linguistically diverse populations.

Here are equity-centered questions for leaders to consider:

- What is equity? Describe a lesson or unit plan with equity learning at its core.
- Do you consider yourself an anti-racist educator? Please explain. What would anti-racism look like in your math, science, ELA, health, art, or social studies curriculum?
- What are some disparities in education today between youth of color and other children? Why do you think they exist? (Answers to these questions will help leaders get to core beliefs.)
- Please describe what you know about people of color's historical excellence and how you would incorporate it into your teaching.
- What scholars' work do you read, and how do you incorporate it into your teaching?
- How do you build sociopolitical consciousness for your professional growth?

- How do you incorporate cultural responsiveness into your practices?
- Typically, curriculum and standards are not written to respond to the identities and histories of youth of color. How might you respond to that fact in your teaching?
- How will you contribute joy to the school building?
- How would you connect teaching content skills to identity, intellect, criticality, and joy?

7. Pre-Plan With Teachers

The HILL Model can be used to observe, evaluate, and support teachers in their practice. Here are questions leaders can ask to fuel pre-teaching discussions with teachers.

- Out of all the topics in the world, why are you teaching this one? (Make sure that teachers know authentic purposes for teaching beyond just following the curriculum guide.)
- Have you checked with students on this topic? What was their feedback?
- How will your unit help students to learn something about themselves or others? *How will identity be taught? How will it be taught and assessed?*
- How will your unit help students to learn new skills? *What standard(s) will be taught? How will it/they be taught and assessed?*
- How will your instruction help students to learn something new? *What knowledge do you hope they will gain? How will it be taught and assessed?*
- How will your instruction help students to learn criticality? *What is your crit topic? How will it be taught and assessed?*
- What multimodal texts will you use to support learning? *What are the anchor texts? What are the layered texts?*
- Are you energized about the teaching and learning? Why?
- How will you make it impossible for students to fail through differentiation, accommodations, and supports?
- In what ways will you change because of the teaching?
- How will your instruction spread and amplify joy? *What is the joy? How will it be taught and assessed?*
- How will your instruction help students to create social change for their communities?

This discussion should lead to a review of the lesson or unit plan and an observation of the teaching. If the leader can't participate in the pre-planning discussion, teams of teachers or coaches can, using these questions. The responses to the questions can help in planning the instruction.

8. Observe and Support Teachers

The HILL Model can be used to guide observations of teachers' unit plans and classroom practice. If you are doing classroom observations, remember, you may not see multiple pursuits on the day you visit the classroom, so it is critical to ask the teacher which pursuit(s) will be taught. Below are questions to consider while reviewing and observing unit plans. They can also be considered while observing student interaction, student artifacts, or assessments.

Identity

- Is this lesson or unit helping students to understand, validate, or celebrate their own identities or the identities of people who are different from them? Can you name the identity or identities being addressed in the teaching?
- What "identity language" is the teacher using?
- What texts is the teacher using to support identity?
- What are the teacher's goals for identity? How is the teacher assessing them?
- What evidence do you see that the teacher has taught identity?
- How are students responding to strategies to build identity?

Skills

- Is this lesson or unit helping students to acquire skills for the content area and grade level? What skills and state standards are being taught?
- What "standards language" is the teacher using?
- What texts is the teacher using to support skills teaching?
- What are the teacher's goals for skills? How is the teacher assessing them?
- What evidence do you see that the teacher has taught skills?
- How are students responding to strategies to build skills?

Intellect

- Is this lesson/unit helping students to know something new about people, places, things, concepts, or events? Can you name the new knowledge being taught?

- How is the teacher helping students to apply skills to new knowledge?
- What "knowledge language" is the teacher using?
- What texts is the teacher using to support intellect?
- What are the teacher's goals for intellect? How is the teacher assessing them?
- What evidence do you see that the teacher has created a space to gain new knowledge?
- How are students responding to strategies to build intellect?

Criticality

- Is this lesson or unit advancing students' understanding of criticality-related topics? Can you name the crit topic being taught?
- What "criticality language" is the teacher using?
- What texts is the teacher using to support criticality?
- What are the teacher's goals for criticality? How is the teacher assessing them?
- What evidence do you see that the teacher has taught criticality?
- How are students responding to strategies to build criticality?

Joy

- Is this lesson or unit advancing students' happiness and joy? Can you name the joy topic being taught?
- Did I feel joyful observing and participating in the instruction?
- What texts is the teaching using to support joy?
- What are the teacher's goals for joy? How is the teacher assessing them?
- What evidence do you see that the teacher taught joy?
- How are students responding to strategies to build joy?

Beyond the five pursuits, leaders can also observe for the teacher:

- connecting with the students—is there concern and care for one another?
- respecting students—and students respecting the teacher
- calling on all students and providing adequate wait time
- giving positive feedback and praising caring, inclusive behavior

The Classroom Environment

- Does your environment have powerful and meaningful quotes from leading writers, artists, and thinkers?
- Does it have up-to-date books in the library and technology?
- Does it showcase student-genius projects?

- listening to students
- inviting discussion about student behavior
- avoiding deficit language with and about students
- encouraging students to construct knowledge
- building on students' interests and linguistic resources
- responding to the identities and histories of students
- tapping into home and community resources
- showing an understanding of students' cultural knowledge
- using interactive and collaborative teaching strategies
- using multimodal texts in instruction
- facilitating learning and learns alongside students
- inviting students to suggest what and how content should be taught
- holding high expectations
- engaging students using a variety of instructional approaches
- creating space for students to voice their ideas and interpretations openly

9. Engage Parents, Caregivers, and Guardians

It is true that students get racist, discriminatory, and sexist ideas from home just as much as they do from media (Internet, television, books, etc.). Therefore, we must engage parents, caregivers, and guardians, and partner with like-minded non-profit organizations, for-profit businesses, and institutions (universities, religious organizations, etc.). I suggest holding at least one program per quarter that benefits parents. Topics can include increasing home literacy, increasing financial literacy, taking advantage of library resources, and so on. Programs should be held at a location in the community other than the school, and preferably planned collaboratively with an established partner in the school or district.

To start, poll community members to see what topics would be beneficial to them, and then invite people in the community who are knowledgeable about that topic to facilitate. The topics and the ways the program is facilitated must help to increase equity, culturally and historically responsive education, inclusion, access, or anti-oppression. To increase parent and community engagement overall, I think parents and community members should be invited into learning about the progress at the school, including data, observations, and meetings. They should be considered equitable efforts of the school.

On the following pages, you'll find examples of ways to use the HILL Model with parents, caregivers, and guardians. The first example contains questions that they can ask their children to check in with them at the end of the school day or week.

> **Identity:** What did you learn about yourself today? What did you learn about other cultures? Do you feel like something caused you to have a stronger and more positive sense of self?
>
> **Skills:** What new skills did you learn today? Do you feel confident in your ability to apply those skills? What do need help with?
>
> **Intellect:** What did you become smarter about today? What do you like to learn about? How does what you learned connect to the real world?
>
> **Criticality:** Did you learn about humanity, problem-solving, or ways to make the world better today? What did you learn about justice? Did your teachers create spaces for self-empowerment? How?
>
> **Joy:** Did you experience joy today? What did you learn that is connected to something beautiful or good in the world?

The next two examples are designed to create home-learning conversations and activities, using musical text.

Music Example: "Entrepreneur," Pharrell Williams featuring JAY-Z
Parents will listen to the song with their child, read the lyrics together, and discuss their meaning. Often children listen to songs without being conscious of what they are about or how they relate to or can help their lives.

Learning Theme: Entrepreneurship

> **Identity:** What is a business that you would love to create?
>
> **Skills:** How much would you have to budget and save?
>
> **Intellect:** What is entrepreneurship?
>
> **Criticality:** What are some of the challenges of starting a business? Are there people who are mistreated or not given fair access to business creation? If so, why do you think this is the case?
>
> **Joy:** How could your business help others and make communities better?

Music Example: "Tomorrow Robins Will Sing," Stevie Wonder
Learning Theme: Social Change and Hope

> **Identity:** What gives you happiness and hope for a better tomorrow?
>
> **Skills:** What would you write to your future self in a letter? What would you want to say? (Youth writes the letter.)
>
> **Intellect:** What does a robin look like? What are some of this bird's characteristics?
>
> **Criticality:** What are the inhumane social conditions that inspired Stevie Wonder to create this song?
>
> **Joy:** Why did Stevie Wonder use the metaphor of a robin to speak of hope for tomorrow?

Current Event Example: New Blue Pigment in Two Centuries: YInMn Blue

> **Identity:** What is your favorite color?
>
> **Skills:** What can you create with this color?
>
> **Intellect:** How was this new pigment discovered?
>
> **Criticality:** How does color make the world better?
>
> **Joy:** What would you name the newest color?

Home Read-Aloud Example: *Nighttime Symphony* by Timbaland and Christopher Myers

> **Identity:** Which sounds are soothing and peaceful to you?
>
> **Skills:** Can you retell the story (including plot, setting, and characters)?
>
> **Intellect:** What is a symphony?
>
> **Criticality:** Why do we need sounds of peace in the world? What are examples of social unrest?
>
> **Joy:** What sounds and songs give beauty in the world?

Video Example: "Ballot or Bullet" (speech) by Malcolm X

Layered Text (quote): "We need more light about each other. Light creates understanding, understanding creates love, love creates patience, and patience creates unity."—Malcolm X

Identity: How am I like Malcolm X?

Skill: What would you say if you wrote your own speech about an important issue? (Youth should write a speech and deliver it to the family.)

Intellect: Who is Malcolm X?

Criticality: Why did Malcolm X speak so much about justice and voting rights?

Joy: What did Malcolm X mean when he said, "We need more light about each other"?

Short Readings Example: "The Wishing Game" (poem) by Annette Browne

Identity: Who do you want to be tomorrow?

Skill: What lyrical story can you write?

Intellect: Who are the people named in the story?

Criticality: Why is it important to have people to look up to? Who do you look up to who teaches you how to love yourself and others?

Joy: What do you wish for?

Parents can also look at images online with their children, talk about what they see, and/or create short stories inspired by the images. I love looking at compelling photographs taken at the end of each year around the world, and asking children to talk about the photographs and write stories or poems.

The Wishing Game
ANNETTE BROWNE

WE gathered 'round the fire last night,
   Jim an' Bess an' me,
And said, "Now let us each in turn
Tell who we'd rather be,
Of all the folks that's in our books."
(Of course, we wouldn't want their looks.)

Bess wished that she'd been Betsy Ross,
The first to make the flag.
One said, "I'd like to do some deed
To make the people brag,
And have the papers print my name,—
If colored girls could rise to fame."

An' I stood out for Roosevelt;
I wished to be like him.
Then Bess said, "We've both had our say,
Now tell who you'd be, Jim."
Jim never thinks like me or Bess,
He knows more than us both, I guess.

He said, "I'd be a Paul Dunbar
Or Booker Washington.
The folks you named were good, I know,
But you see, Tom, each one
Of these two men I'd wish to be
Were colored boys, like you and me.

10. Question University Syllabi

Lastly, what does this work look like at the university level? Rather than thinking about a single course on culturally responsive pedagogy, consider what all the courses in each program could look like if they all aimed to help students learn about who they are and about the cultural lives of others, learn skills and pedagogical methods, learn new content and theories, learn about justice, anti-racism, and equity, and learn to love themselves and find joy in the profession. This would make for more holistic programs and could begin to reshape who become teachers, how they are prepared, and whether, when they have completed their coursework, they are ready to move into any type of classrooms. Doing equity work at the university level doesn't come without its challenges. There are times when anti-racism and equity work, and its heaviness, falls upon those few professors of color. There are also frequent reports of Black professors receiving anti-Black and other racist comments on their evaluations. This work must be infused into the whole program and not just a component of it. As I prepare my course syllabi, these are questions that I walk myself through:

- How can the course develop students' identities, skills, intellect, criticality, and joy?
- Are students reading works by diverse authors?
- Are students reading multimodal texts (and not just articles and books)?
- Are students reading and learning theories of people of color?
- Are students learning criticality?
- Are assignments pushing students to think about, understand, and disrupt oppression?
- Are policies making it impossible for students to fail?
- Are policies written with critical love as a priority?
- How do the five pursuits show up explicitly on the syllabus?
- How are the five pursuits taught and assessed on the syllabus?
- How is my content connected to students' lives?
- Am I energized to teach and for my students to learn?
- Have I done the things I'm asking my students to do?
- Does my instruction reflect my students' histories, identities, literacies, and liberation? How?

This is just a starter list of questions. It is key that college faculty establish criteria for each course that is grounded in the work of equity, justice, and cultural and historical responsiveness. I also use the pursuits to ground my planning and student goals for college courses, such as the goals I present below for an undergraduate course on Stevie Wonder's musicality.

Conversation Peace: Exploring the Music of Stevie Wonder

Identity: Students will compare the social messages in Stevie Wonder's music to their own lives.

Skills: Students will learn how to study, code, and interrogate song lyrics, so they aren't passive consumers of media.

Intellect: Students will learn about Stevie Wonder, his music, and his artistry.

Criticality: Students will explore resistance and social change through Stevie Wonder's music.

Joy: Students will learn the joy of musicality.

"Art Is a Powerful Tool"

Emory Douglas is a graphic artist who was named the Minister of Culture and Revolutionary Artist of the Black Panther Party. Like many artists, his creations connected to life, honesty, and criticality. He and his art were bold, unapologetic, and powerful and left our minds better. I appreciate his Manifesto because it reminds me that programs and initiatives that we create for our schools become our own *form of art*.

**POLITICAL ARTIST MANIFESTO:
(Food for thought)**

1- Don't be fooled by deception.

2- Don't be deceitful or corruptible.

3- Know you get more truth from the artists than from bureaucrats.

4- Recognize that art is a powerful tool a language that can be used to Enlighten, Inform, a guide to Actions.

5- Create art that Recognizes the Oppression of Others, and considers basic quality of life concerns and basic human rights issues.

6- Create art of social concerns that even a child can understand.

7- The goal should always be to Make the Message Clear.

8- Make an effort not to create political art dealing with social issues just because it's a a cool thing to do.

9- Create art that Challenges the Colonization of the Imagination.

10- Self evaluate ones work, and be open to constructive evaluations from others, be open to making adjustments if you choose to do so and be prepared if necessary to defend and explain what you communicate through your art.

11- Know the rules before you break the rules.

12- Do not loose sight of what the goals are.

We have learned that education development is artistic, and, much the same way that Emory Douglas describes the artist's declaration, leaders can make a similar declaration. I leave you, dear leaders, with this very challenge. How can your leadership feel like art and embark upon these same 12 elements in the Manifesto? And how do we work to never "lose sight of what the goals are," which include watering this earth by working to advance humanity and our children within it?

Chapter 6 Reflection

Select one or more questions to engage in a freewrite.

- What are some reactions and reflections you have about the music, art, and text from Chapter 6?
- What ideas and passages stand out for you, and why?
- What parts do you want to explore and learn about more?
- What parts of the educational system have helped you to grow?
- Which parts of the educational system are in need of water?
- What do you plan to do to unearth genius and joy?

Take some time to color this image.

CHAPTER 7

Planting Seeds for the Future:

Artistic Interpretations of the HILL Model

Artwork by children at The Williamsburg High School of Art and Technology in Brooklyn, New York. The school leader, Cara Tait, alongside her incredible team and artist, Misha Tyutyunik, gathered classes of children to engage in interpreting the pursuits of the HILL Model. I noticed how the children did not create a piece on skills—perhaps they wanted to illuminate the less-centered other pursuits. Each artful expression tells a story of genius, joy, resistance, and excellence. It captures the meaning of the pursuit visually, without print. This is genius. These are our children.

> "There is always a light, if only we're brave enough to see it. If only we're brave enough to be it."
>
> —AMANDA GORMAN

My People
by Langston Hughes

The night is beautiful,
So the faces of my people.

The stars are beautiful,
So the eyes of my people.

Beautiful, also, is the sun.
Beautiful, also, are the souls of my people.

Bouquet
by Langston Hughes

Gather quickly
Out of darkness
All the songs you know
And throw them at the sun
Before they melt
Like snow.

Unearthing Thought

1. How does it feel to congregate and collaborate with conscious colleagues and youth?

2. How do you know when you see excellence in teaching and learning?

3. Why do some people feel it is more difficult to implement CHRE in some grades and content areas than others? What do you feel is difficult? Less difficult?

4. How do students respond to the joy of teaching and learning?

5. How would you continue to strive for CHRE in spaces where you feel intellectually constrained?

6. What does educational freedom mean to you?

7. What do educational and curricular reparations mean to you?

8. Why are models and mentors of teaching and learning important?

9. How do you celebrate yourself, students, and colleagues when you share genius?

10. What beautiful gift will you share with the world next?

Centering Artistic Genius

This chapter is a display of creative works submitted by teachers and leaders, many of whom I have worked closely with, coaching them through the process of culturally and historically responsive education. Yet, it feels more than a display to me—it feels like a "bouquet" of glorious flowers delivered from "my people" to the world. These are educators who continually strive for better, more equitable education. Their works show what educators can do when they are not constrained intellectually or prohibited from putting truth to power—from infusing the classroom with joy. These educators are bravely paving a new way forward, often working against pressures, racism, and basic/mediocre structures. This forward movement has felt like light. As Amanda Gorman expressed, "there is always light"—always a new way of teaching, learning, and living, but it takes courage to see it and be it. It takes dismantling, rebuilding, and disrupting the norms that have not served us well.

Although this chapter is organized by grade level, please do not feel constrained by the level or levels you teach. Review all of the instructional ideas and adapt them as necessary to meet the needs and interests of your students. The gallery covers various content areas as well. Certainly, there are more examples of excellent work that is not displayed here. To find them, go to scholastic.com/UnearthingJoyResources.

PreK–K

Lesson Plans: Identity Read-Alouds

Featured Teaching Artist: Charnea Paris, Bronx, New York

Your Name Is a Song by Jamilah Thompkins-Bigelow

Identity: I can learn that every name comes from some special place (families, songs, poems).

Skills: I can retell the story and share information from the text during class discussions or small-group activities.

Intellect: I can learn about the meaning of my name and my classmates' names.

Criticality: I can learn that one way of showing respect to others and myself is learning to pronounce names and teaching others to pronounce my name correctly.

Joy: I can feel joy, love, and excitement as I say and hear my name called or spoken.

The Day You Begin by Jacqueline Woodson

Identity: I can name something that makes me unique.

Skills: I can describe the characters in the story.

Intellect: I can learn about the concept of diversity.

Criticality: I can learn the importance of diversity and the beauty in difference.

Joy: I can find joy in being able to share with friends who are just like me.

"There are those who give with joy, and that joy is their reward."

—KHALIL GIBRAN

Math Play Center Activities

These activities extend the *Your Name Is a Song* identity read-aloud lesson, adding the skills of measuring with different units, patterning, graphing, and sorting.

- **How Long Is My Name?:** Students measure their names using counting cubes, and pipe cleaners in various sizes.
- **How Many Letters?:** Students graph how many letters are in their names.

These activities extend *The Day You Begin* identity read-aloud lesson, adding the skills of patterning, measuring, and sorting.

- **Let's Make a Pattern:** Students make a pattern with beads of various colors.
- **Look How Tall I Am:** Students use a piece of yarn or string to measure each other to see how tall they are.
- **My Body Color Sorting:** Take pictures of each student's hands and allow children to sort them into cups by the various skin colors they see.

Science Play Center Activities

These activities extend *The Day You Begin* identity read-aloud lesson, adding the skills of comparing and contrasting features of different varieties of the same fruit.

- **Not the Color of Our Skin:** Students compare shapes, colors, and sizes of different varieties of apples. Teachers cut the apples in half and share with students that no matter the shape, color, or size there is always a core with seeds in the shape of a star at the center. They help students draw the comparison between these apples and a group of kids.
- **My Fingerprints Are One of a Kind:** Students make and study their own prints to find a unique pattern and to find some similarities with classmates' prints.

Grades 1–2

Lesson Plan: Culturally and Historically Responsive ELA Using *The Proudest Blue*

Featured Teaching Artist: Alexandria Lopez, Bushwick, New York

Identity: Students will think of their own families and artifacts that represent their own culture.

Skills: Students will describe the author's point of view and identify who the speaker is and how the narrator feels, using key details about events in the text.

Intellect: Students will learn what a hijab is and its significance in the Muslim community.

Criticality: Students will recognize the obstacles the main character and her sister face because of the sister's hijab and brainstorm solutions to problem-solve and respond to hate, bullying, and social and cultural diversity.

Joy: Students will create an art piece that conveys what brings them joy and makes them unique.

"Don't carry around the hurtful words that others say. Drop them. They are not yours to keep. They belong only to those who said them."

—from *The Proudest Blue* by Ibtihaj Muhammad, with S.K. Ali

Lesson Plan: Celebrating Our Identities Through Poetry

Featured Teaching Artist: Stacey Joy, Los Angeles, California

Identity: Students will become more aware of their identities and their classmates' identities by honoring what they can learn, do, and become.

Skills: Students will use the mentor poem "Hey Black Child" by Useni Eugene Perkins to write their own poem about what they can learn, do, and become. They will recite their poems to a larger audience.

Intellect: Students will learn how each of us has unique identities and characteristics.

Criticality: Students will find similarities in their classmates' identities (what they like to learn, do, or become) and identify how they show up in the world and will show up in the future. They will share strengths in their identities that will serve as tools in fighting oppression.

Joy: Students will express self-love and joy through poetry.

Lesson Plan: *Something Beautiful*

Featured Teaching Artist: Tracy Pharris, Los Angeles, California

Read aloud *Something Beautiful* by Sharon Dennis Wyeth

Identity: Students will answer the question, *Where do I live?*, and take a walk around their neighborhood with an adult.

Skills: Students will describe what they see and why it is beautiful to them.

Intellect: Students will define what makes a neighborhood.

Criticality: Students will learn ways to protect and sustain their neighborhoods.

Joy: Students will find something beautiful in their neighborhood and capture it through art and/or writing.

Standards Addressed

- Tell a story or recount an experience with appropriate facts and relevant, descriptive details, speaking audibly in coherent sentences.

- Create audio recordings of stories or poems; add drawings or other visual displays to stories or recounts of experiences when appropriate to clarify ideas, thoughts, and feelings.

- Produce complete sentences when appropriate to the task and situation in order to provide requested details or clarification.

- Write opinion pieces in which they introduce the topic or book they are writing about, state an opinion, supply reasons that support the opinion, use linking words (e.g., *because, and, also*) to connect opinion and reasons, and provide a concluding statement or section).

Grades 3–5

Unit Plan: Seeing More Stars

Featured Teaching Artists: Leonard Aylward, Erik Teather, Sonja Upton, Kim Salierno, Rob Dunlop, Tiffney Petrucci, and Kristia Penlington, DSBN, Ontario

Identity: Students will think about how different communities observe the stars and how access issues/barriers to visibility/sky-viewing might vary by community.

Skills: Students will participate in collaborative conversations with diverse partners about stars and draw inferences from a variety of literary, graphic, and informational texts (ELA). They will learn about light pollution (Science).

Intellect: Students will investigate how sky-viewing is impacted by various technologies, taking different perspectives into account and how in some areas, it has become harder to see the stars at night. They will learn about cities with high and low light pollution levels.

Criticality: Students will reflect on barriers and access in different communities and the implications of light pollution on wildlife and nature. They will select one of those issues and develop an action plan.

Joy: Students will experience the joy, beauty, and wonder of the stars and the environment.

Family/Home Connection: Invite families to:

- Share personal stories about the stars.
- Plan a family stargazing experience. Encourage them to compare what they see to what they find at theskylive.com.
- Investigate books, photos, apps, or videos of the night sky, and share their discoveries and wonderings.
- Visit a planetarium.
- Take a photograph of light pollution in their community and bring it to school to show to the class.

Unit Plan: Bees/*Las Abejas*

Featured Teaching Artist: Lara J. Handsfield, Normal, Illinois

Identity: Students will examine the role of bees in their own lives (e.g., working in the fields, family gardens, etc.)

Skills:

- **Vocabulary:** Students will explore cross-linguistic connections (e.g., cognates) pertaining to bees: nectar/*el néctar*, pollen/*el polen*, pollination/*la polinización*, melittologist/*la melitólogo*, beekeeping/*apicultura*, beekeeper/*la apicultora*.
- **Spelling:** Students will analyze and compare double-consonant digraphs in both English and Spanish (*-ll*, *-tt*, *-zz*) and double-vowel digraphs in English (*-ee*, *-oo*), comparing them with vowels and vowel sounds in Spanish (*i*, *u*).

Intellect: Students will learn about the following topics, which cover math, social studies, and science:

- Traditions of beekeeping among Mayan cultures
- Bee intelligence and the life of a hive
- Plants/flowers that attract bees and sustain bee communities

Criticality: Students will inquire into the role of bees in healthy ecologies and the effects of climate change and/or industrial farming on bee populations. They will also connect hierarchies in bee communities to hierarchies in human communities, including labor practices.

Joy: Students will prepare and enjoy foods sweetened with honey.

Layered Texts

- *Bee Love (Can Be Hard)* by Alan Page and Kamie Page
- *The King of Bees* by Lester L. Laminack
- *Honeybee: The Busy Life of Apis Mellifera* by Candace Fleming
- *El Baile de las Abejas* por Fran Nuño
- *The Last Cuentista* by Donna Barba Higuera (novel, final chapters)
- *La Abeja de Más/One Bee Too Many* by Andrés Pi Andreu (Latin American fable)
- Nuevo estudio demuestra que las abejas melíferas pueden resolver problemas matemáticos básicos (NewsELA article)
- "America's Last Honeybee Food Refuge Is Disappearing" (NewsELA article)
- Honey Hard Candy (recipe)
- "Xunankab Bee Honey (Melipona Beecheii)," Slow Food Presidia, Yucatán, Mexico (YouTube video)

Grades 6–8

Unit Plan: Color Our World

Featured Teaching Artists: Kim Bergsma, Jason Eckhardt, Katie Lagerwerf, Carey McLean, Susan Plat, and Ann Rigg, DSBN, Ontario

Identity: Students will explain how skin color is unique and how our individual differences need to be celebrated each and every day.

Skills: Students will learn about cultural differences and skin color, including how melanin impacts skin tone. They will answer questions based on various texts and identify the audience and the author's intended purpose/message.

Intellect: Students will learn about pigmentation and melanin, and define beauty from different perspectives.

Criticality: Students will think critically and discuss colorism and how some skin tones have led to oppression. They will consider other aspects in our world that need to evolve in their inclusivity and representation.

Joy: Students will learn how all skin tones are beautiful.

Layered Texts

- *The Colors of Us* by Karen Katz
- *Sulwe* by Lupita Nyong'o
- The Science of Skin Color (TED-Ed video)
- "Brown Skin Girl" song by Beyoncé, Blue Ivy, SAINt JHN, Wizkid

In this unit plan, teachers problematize historic names of crayon colors, such as "flesh," and students critique those names to determine if they are inclusive or oppressive. Students learn the importance of seeing oneself and being able to draw oneself with appropriate and available materials. The class studies child crayon activist Bellen Woodard, and looks at the history of the Crayola company across the years. They extend their learning by researching companies and their products to see how sensitive they are to the skin color of Black and Brown people. Students hold a fundraiser to raise money for inclusive products, such as crayons and bandages, and calculate the expenses and income from the fundraiser.

Unit Plan: The Mathematics of Fresh and Healthy Food

Identity: Students will calculate the distance to fresh and healthy food across various communities in Chicago.

Skills: Students will problem-solve using data sets. They will collect and plot data related to food security in their community.

Intellect: Students will learn about food security.

Criticality: Students will examine food apartheid and food deserts, and research communities that have access to healthy and fresh food.

Joy: Students will learn the benefits of fresh and healthy food to the body.

Family/Home Connection: Families can calculate the distances to fresh and healthy food across their community, city, or town.

Unit Plan: Hear My Voice/*Escucha mi voz*: Immigration Reform From the Perspective of Young Immigrants

Featured Teaching Artist: Courtney Wai, San Antonio, Texas

Read aloud *Hear My Voice/Escucha mi voz: The Testimonies of Children Detained at the Southern Border of the United States* by Warren Binford

Identity: Students will think of themselves as leaders who can contribute ideas to immigration reform because of their personal experiences.

Skills: Students will write an argumentative paper using evidence from articles, documentaries, their personal experience, and discussion with immigration leaders and activists. Students can write and speak across languages.

Intellect: Students will participate in a discourse with immigration experts and share their ideas for immigration reform.

Criticality: Students will explore the barriers that undocumented immigrants face and ways immigrants' activism addresses those barriers.

Joy: Students will develop solutions based on their own experiences and the activism of other immigrant communities.

Grades 9–12

Unit Plan: Dance Feminism

Featured Teaching Artist: DeAngelo Blanchard, New York, New York

Identity: Students will reflect on how mundane tasks have an impact on one's character. They will also reflect on their roles and responsibilities within society.

Skills: Students will utilize gestures inspired by everyday tasks that they engage with in order to generate and create a dance study.

Intellect: Students will learn about the effects of societal norms toward women and what those norms may yield for different people who interact with them, especially Black women.

Criticality: Students will identify the ways in which Black women have been seen in American society and how those roles can be celebrated or used to dehumanize them.

Joy: Students will acknowledge their own embodied histories and appreciate the various skills that they already have, know, and can contribute beyond the dance room.

Layered Texts

- photos of women in various roles in society
- Michelle Obama's Manchester, New Hampshire, speech, October 13, 2016
- various household tools and supplies

Unit Plan: Ethics of Nuclear Technologies

Featured Teaching Artists: Amanda Sparhawk, Natasha Singh, and Faven Habte, Chicago, Illinois

Identity: Students will develop an understanding of their personal values when making ethical decisions. They will demonstrate an understanding of those who hold different opinions and use these perspectives to inform their own beliefs.

Skills: Students will develop models to illustrate the changes in the composition of the nucleus of the atom during radioactive decay. They will use models and mathematical techniques to explain the scale and impact of energy changes in nuclear processes. They will analyze data and use mathematical representations of half-life to explain how the radioactive decay of materials can affect society.

Intellect: Students will learn about nuclear energy and nuclear weapons to take a stance on whether they should be used.

Criticality: Students will critically analyze who has the power to use nuclear power plants and weapons versus who may feel the negative effects of their use.

Joy: Students will examine how advocacy for the rights of others contributes to the common good.

Chapter 7 Reflection

Why do we all do this beautiful work in education, if not for the dreams, potential, and joy of our youth—our students? They are who we are accountable to before our supervisors, principals, superintendents, and school board members. They rely on us to show up always in forms of joyous excellence. Our students expect us to guide them toward their dreams and aspirations. To do that, our curriculum, our teaching, and their learning must be guided by the earth, by nature, by life, and by humanity. It may feel natural to feel deflated and defeated by a system that fails to center genius, justice, and joy. But we see again and again, hope. The genius of our village shows up when we grow tired of fighting for excellence. It is that collectivism that keeps us going—keeps us dreaming—toward joy. Joy, as defined in this book, must always be the goal of education. It must be our work.

"Youth is a beautiful dream, on whose brightness books shed a blinding dust. Will ever the day come when the wise link the joy of knowledge to youth's dream? Will ever the day come when Nature becomes the teacher of man, humanity his book and life his school? Youth's joyous purpose cannot be fulfilled until that day comes."

—KHALIL GIBRAN

Take some time to color this image.

Afterword: Joy as Magic and Infinite Possibilities

I Dream a World
by Langston Hughes

I dream a world where man
No other man will scorn,
Where love will bless the earth
And peace its paths adorn.
I dream a world where all
Will know sweet freedom's way,
Where greed no longer saps the soul
Nor avarice blights our day.
A world I dream where black or white,
Whatever race you be,
Will share the bounties of the earth
And every man is free,
Where wretchedness will hang its head
And joy, like a pearl,
Attends the needs of all mankind—
Of such I dream, my world!

When writing this book, I thought about the importance of sight and vision—two things Stevie Wonder deeply has regarding the world. He is able to tell stories and see the world in ways that felt magical to me growing up. I wanted to embody his creativity and artfulness in my own pathway as an educator. I have always loved the song "If It's Magic." It allowed me to dream up a world of wonder, possibility, and sustained freedom and joy. The song put me in a state of peace and relaxation. I felt a "calm joy" that the earth will be taken care of.

I feel what education can be. It can be genius. It can feel *everlasting, pleasing, never leaving, timeless, special,* as if it's *keeping danger from a child,* and there is certainly *enough for everyone* to have their lives honored in curriculum and instruction. After writing this book I heard this song differently. Every time Stevie Wonder used the word *it,* I replaced it in my mind with the word *joy.*

Listen to "If It's Magic," Stevie Wonder.

Isn't that the goal of education? Joy as magic and infinite possibilities… as brilliance and excitement where we return each day, different, better… smiling… our thirst for knowledge and a thirst to be better for our children. I thought about joy leaving *no heart undone*.

My Dear Educators,

I have one desire for the state of our system of education and as individual teachers, leaders, community, and staff who work within our schools each day. My desire for you is that you center and carry forth your genius, because it requires our specificity today and tomorrow.

When you are tired and overwhelmed as you cultivate (and water) the next generations, please remember to claim and reclaim your joy over and over again and (re)member the very purpose of why you entered this beautiful field of education. It is my hope that you rely on the same practices that you instill within your children involving art, music, multimodalities, creativity, and intellectualism. Take moments to be still, to rest, to love yourselves and one another. (Re)member that the ancestors did not "wait on" or "rely on" anyone for justice or to engage in righteousness for children. While we are urgently pushing forth toward a better system, we must (now) shift to and extend the types of pedagogies that will not just give our students access to elevated parts of their lives, but will also give them joy—experiencing the full beauty of the sun—for *there is enough for everyone*.

To you, with love, justice, and joy to this earth,

—GHOLDY

Take some time to color this image.

References

Adichie, C. N. (2009, July). The danger of a single story [Transcript]. TED Conferences.

Banks, J. A. (1999). *An introduction to multicultural education (2nd ed.).* Allyn and Bacon.

Barry, A. L. (2008). Reading the past: Historical antecedents to contemporary reading methods and materials. *Reading Horizons, 49*(1), 31–52.

Bishop, R. S. (1990). Mirrors, windows, and sliding glass doors. *Perspectives, 1*(3), ix–xi.

Brooks, W. M., & McNair, J. C. (Eds.). (2008). *Embracing, evaluating, and examining African American children's and young adult literature.* The Scarecrow Press.

Brown, D. N. (2011, July 8). Afro-Colombian women braid messages of freedom in hairstyles. *Washington Post.* Retrieved May 5, 2022, from washingtonpost.com/lifestyle/style/afro-colombian-women-braid-messages-of-freedom-in-hairstyles/2011/07/08/gIQA6X9W4H_story.html?utm_term=.361bf64bc666.

Bryan-Gooden, J., Hester, M. & Peoples, L. Q. (2019). *Culturally responsive curriculum scorecard.* Metropolitan Center for Research on Equity and the Transformation of Schools, New York University.

Case, S. H. (2002). The historical ideology of Mildred Lewis Rutherford: A Confederate historian's New South creed. *The Journal of Southern History, 68*(3), 599–628.

Cooper, A. (2009). *My name is Phillis Wheatley: A story of slavery and freedom.* Kids Can Press.

Dillard, C. B. (2022). *The spirit of our work: Black women teachers (re)member.* Beacon Press.

Du Bois, W. E. B. (1920). Darkwater: Voices from within the veil. Harcourt, Brace and Howe.

Du Bois, W. E. B. (1919). The true brownies. *The Crisis: A Record of the Darker Races, 18,* 285–86.

Dunbar, E. A. (2019). *She came to slay: The life and times of Harriet Tubman.* 37 Ink.

Dunbar-Ortiz, R., Mendoza, J. (Adapter), & Reese, D. (Adapter). (2019). *An Indigenous peoples' history of the United States for young people.* Beacon Press.

Foster, G. (2004, January 21). *History of the historically Black independent schools in New York City 1704–2020.* AHBIS. Retrieved March 5, 2022, from ahbis.org/copy-of-history

Gay, G. (2010). *Culturally responsive teaching: Theory, research, and practice, 2nd edition.* Teachers College Press.

Gee, J. P. (2001). Reading as situated language: A sociocognitive perspective. *Journal of Adolescent & Adult Literacy, 44*(8), 714–725.

Geraty, V. M. (1997). *Gulluh fuh oonuh (Gullah for you): A guide to the Gullah language.* Sandlapper Pub. Co.

Gilio-Whitaker, D. (2019). *As long as grass grows: The Indigenous fight for environmental justice, from colonization to Standing Rock.* Beacon Press.

Hale, J. (2011). The student as a force for social change: The Mississippi Freedom Schools and student engagement. *The Journal of African American History, 96*(3), 325–347.

Hannah-Jones, N., Roper, C., Silverman, I., & Silverstein, J. (2021). *The 1619 project: A new American origin story.* WH Allen, an imprint of Ebury Publishing.

Harris, V. J. (1989). Race consciousness, refinement, and radicalism: Socialization in the Brownies' book. *Children's Literature Association Quarterly, 14*(4), 192–96.

Huyck, D., & Dahlen, S. P. (2019 June 19). *Diversity in children's books 2018.* sarahpark.com blog. Created in consultation with Edith Campbell, Molly Beth Griffin, K. T. Horning, Debbie Reese, Ebony Elizabeth Thomas, and Madeline Tyner, with statistics compiled by the Cooperative Children's Book Center, School of Education, University of Wisconsin-Madison: Retrieved from readingspark.wordpress.com/2019/06/19/picture-this-diversity-in-childrens-books-2018-infographic.

Ladson-Billings, G. (1994). *The dreamkeepers: Successful teachers of African American children.* Jossey-Bass.

Ladson-Billings, G. (2014). Culturally relevant pedagogy 2.0: a.k.a. the remix. *Harvard Educational Review, 84*(1), 74–84.

Ladson-Billings, G. (2021). *Culturally relevant pedagogy: Asking a different question.* Teachers College Press.

Lerman, S. (2000). The social turn in mathematics education research. *Multiple Perspectives on Mathematics Teaching and Learning,* 19–44.

Loewen, J. W. (2014). *Lies my teacher told me about Christopher Columbus: What your history books got wrong.* The New Press.

Lorde, A. (1984/2020) *Sister outsider: Essays and speeches.* Penguin Random Group.

McIlwain, G. (1995). *Tut language.* Tut Language Co.

Muhammad, G. (2020). *Cultivating genius: An equity model for culturally and historically responsive literacy.* Scholastic.

Muhammad, G. E., & Moodie, C. (2022). A model for equity and access: Teaching adolescent literacy from a Black historical lens. In K. A. Hinchman (Ed.), *Best practices in adolescent literacy instruction.* Guilford.

National Council of Teachers of English (NCTE). (2020). NCTE position paper on the role of English teachers in educating English language learners, March 6, 2020. https://ncte.org/statement/teaching-english-ells/

Oxford University Press. (2019). *Oxford Dictionary of Biology.*

Rutherford, M. L., & United Confederate Veterans. (1920). *A measuring rod to test text books, and reference books in schools, colleges, and libraries.* United Confederate Veterans.

Saad, E. N. (2010). *Social history of Timbuktu: The role of Muslim scholars and notables, 1400–1900.* Cambridge University Press.

Schaeffer, K. (2021, December 10). America's public school teachers are far less racially and ethnically diverse than their students. Retrieved January 4, 2022, from pewresearch.org/fact-tank/2021/12/10/americas-public-school-teachers-are-far-less-racially-and-ethnically-diverse-than-their-students/

Schomburg Center for Research in Black Culture, Manuscripts, Archives and Rare Books Division, The New York Public Library. Andrews, C. C. (1830). *The history of the New-York African free-schools, from their establishment in 1787, to the present time.* Retrieved from digitalcollections.nypl.org/items/510d47e4-123b-a3d9-e040-e00a18064a99

Sealey-Ruiz, Y. (2022). An archaeology of self for our times: Another talk to teachers. *English Journal, 111*(5), 21–26.

Singleton, B. D. (2004). African bibliophiles: Books and libraries in medieval Timbuktu. *Libraries & Culture, 39*(1), 1–12.

Tatum, B. D. (2003). *"Why are all the Black kids sitting together in the cafeteria?": And other conversations about race.* BasicBooks.

U.S. Department of Education. Institute of Education Sciences, National Center for Education Statistics, National Assessment of Educational Progress (NAEP), 2022 Reading and Mathematics Assessments.

Watson-Vandiver, M. J., & Wiggan, G. (2021). *The healing power of education: Afrocentric pedagogy as a tool for restoration and liberation.* Teachers College Press.

Wheatley, P., Livermore, G., Force, P., Ingraham, E. D., Jefferson Exhibit Collection & John Davis Batchelder Collection. (1773). Poems on various subjects, religious and moral. [Printed for A. Bell, bookseller, Aldgate and sold by Messrs. Cox and Berry] Retrieved from the Library of Congress, https://www.loc.gov/item/30020911/.

Willis, A. I., & Harris, V. J. (2000). Political acts: Literacy learning and teaching. *Reading Research Quarterly, 35*(1), 72–88.

Index